# RTC

D1555026

# PARTNERS AT HOME AND AT WORK

# PARTNERS AT HOME AND AT WORK
## How couples can build a successful business together without killing each other

Annette O'Shea-Roche
Sieglinde Malmberg

**Self-Counsel Press**
(*a division of*)
International Self-Counsel Press Ltd.
Canada    U.S.A.

Printed in Canada

First edition: October, 1994


Canadian Cataloguing in Publication Data
O'Shea-Roche, Annette, 1961-
    Partners at home and at work

    (Self-counsel business series)
    ISBN 0-88908-521-8

    1. Couple-owned business enterprises — Management.
2. Work and family.   I. Malmberg, Sieglinde.   II. Title.
III. Series
HD62.27.O83   1994       658.02'2'08655      C94-910787-5


Cover photo by Terry Guscott, ATN Visuals, Vancouver, B.C.




**Self-Counsel Press**
(*a division of*)
International Self-Counsel Press Ltd.

1481 Charlotte Road                1704 N. State Street
North Vancouver, British Columbia  Bellingham, Washington
V7J 1H1                            98225

# CONTENTS

# WORKSHEETS

# CHECKLISTS

# SAMPLES

# INTRODUCTION

This book came into being because of our observations and experiences from running our own businesses. In our work with Annette's company, W.I.S.E. (Women in Successful Enterprises), we ran a program for women entrepreneurs to improve their bottom line through effective management of their capital and human resources. As we worked on-site with these women, the impact of the influence of their partners/spouses often became apparent. Sometimes their spouses worked directly with them in the business or were their "not-so-silent-partners" or "supporters." It was not unusual to have a participant in the program delay a business decision until she could receive input from her spouse, whether he was active in the business or not. Sometimes the delays and the surrounding communication problems that emerged had a serious negative impact on the success of the business.

Sieglinde was also working with larger corporations. She began to realize how many corporations were family- or couple-oriented. The majority of challenges faced by these companies were human ones. Many of these stemmed from the inability of the founding couple to clarify their roles in the business. The confusion spilled over into the ranks of the employees, in one case to such an extent that the business went bankrupt.

As we explored the apparent problem, our research showed that over 47% of North American small businesses and corporations are run by couples. About 80% of home-based businesses and 60% to 70% of all franchises are run by couples. Many franchise owners we met who ran the business with their spouse described the challenges they were facing. We met couples working together in network marketing, who, while they received training and support in how to increase their network, hadn't received any help with the challenge of being a couple in business together. Both of us work with our husbands in our respective businesses, so we could relate to the issues these couples described.

When we combined our observations with the failure rate statistics for small businesses, we realized that the chances of a couple or family running a successful business were slim, unless they received some guidance and business advice before they began, or at least in the very early stages of their business life.

As a trend began to emerge, we designed a workshop for couple entrepreneurs and called it "Love Me, Love My Business." The goal of our two-and-a-half day workshop was to help couples anticipate potential problems and create solutions before problems arose. The changes in the couples who attended our workshops were dramatic. Tensions were dissipated as each person was allowed to claim a portion of the business as his or her responsibility. The couples learned to recognize each other's strengths and weaknesses and to design systems and procedures to ensure that the work got done, even during a family crisis. We also met couples who decided as a result of the workshop that they should not be working together, or that the jobs they had taken in the company were not the ones they wanted. Some couples very painfully came to the conclusion that they could not work together, but as a result of the workshop, they decided that they could stay together as a family.

There is very little training that prepares us for running a business. Most people go into business because they have a good idea and want to run with it. There is also no training to help people prepare for being in a relationship. Our backgrounds, upbringing, and life experience have everything to do with how we contribute to the success of a partnership, whether it is business or personal. We were fortunate to work with some couples who were just beginning their business ventures and with others who had accumulated many years of frustration. The issues described in this book are ones that surfaced again and again in our workshops.

We have structured our book very much along the lines of our workshop. We begin by examining the scope of the problem. Couples must realize that they are not alone. There are millions of businesses in North America, all at different stages of development.

First, with each stage of growth, couples face different decisions and challenges. The business inventory worksheet we introduce in this book has been designed to help you analyze which stage your business is at and how each of your strengths and weaknesses contributes to the success of the business.

We also found that a problem couples often face is lack of role definition or "who does what." Job descriptions are essential in business and especially for the founding couple. The job description worksheets in chapter 4 can help you pinpoint all the tasks that are essential to running your business and running your life.

Another problem couples may not anticipate is disagreement and conflict. Couples need strategies for resolving conflicts. There are going to be times when you will disagree. This book offers methods to let you do that as efficiently as possible.

Conflict often arises for couples because of decisions one partner has made for the business. This book can help both of you analyze and understand each other's decision-making style and maximize your strengths. Each partner must be fully informed and aware of what is going on in the business.

Knowing when and how to delegate tasks is also a problem couples face. For the sake of the business, couples must be prepared to pass on duties to employees. Those employees must be properly trained and fully aware of what they must do. From what couples told us, problems often arose because of one partner's hasty and inadequate delegation of duties.

Couples who have children face all these problems and the task of meeting their children's needs as well. There are ways to balance family and business life, even when your business is based in your home. Couples must consider the effect of having Mommy and Daddy run a business.

However, despite all your care and attention or perhaps the lack of it, you may not be able to resolve your differences. What happens if your relationship ends? What happens to your business? Can you still work together? Chapter 8 offers ways for couples to dissolve their business relationship without destroying the business.

Throughout the book we have adapted our clients' stories and used them to illustrate the problems that couple entrepreneurs face. It was a privilege and a pleasure to work with so many couples who are dedicated entrepreneurs and committed to a new style of living and working. Whether they chose to go into business or not, the couples we met were courageously trying to build businesses and lives that reflected their beliefs, values, and shared goals. We salute them and thank them all for their contribution to this book.

# 1

## COUPLES AS PARTNERS: A CONTINUING TREND

### a. THE RISE OF THE COUPLE-OWNED BUSINESS

In the last 20 years, there has been an astounding rise in the number of entrepreneurial couples starting businesses in North America. There are several factors behind this rise, and there is no sign that it will slow down.

The first factor has been the change in fortunes of many large North American corporations. In the face of international competition, some companies have had to lay off thousands of workers, downsize operations, flatten management layers, contract out, and close plants to maintain their competitive edge. When long-time employees are laid off, many companies have been able to offer fair and reasonable financial settlements. These lump sum payments now allow people some flexibility in choosing a new career. The choice often has been to open a business. The next choice is to open the business with the person closest to them, their spouse or partner.

A second factor in the rise of couple-owned businesses is the growing acceptance of the idea of running your own business. The image of the corporation as the most desirable employer has changed. Universities and colleges across North America now offer courses in entrepreneurial skills, something that was unheard of even in the late eighties. The pursuit of happiness seems more and more tied to personal, rather than corporate, success.

Technology has advanced to the point that it is not only feasible, but practical to run a business from home. This has created a boom in the number of home-based businesses in North America. While some home-based businesses are run by one person, an estimated 80% are couple-owned and operated. Even those that are "owned" by one partner get the benefit of ideas, financial support, and time from the other partner, and often from the children.

The women's movement is another contributor to the rise of entrepreneurial couples. Statistics tell us that by the year 2000, as much as 70% of the work force in North America will be female. Women differ from men in what they want from work and in their expectations that work will form part of the whole of their lives, not necessarily become its sole focus. Corporate employers have not met the needs of women, so many women have chosen to open their own businesses.

Two more powerful business trends have added to the rise of entrepreneurial couples. Franchising and network marketing are accepted as driving forces for economic growth, and an estimated 60% to 70% of franchises and network marketing businesses are owned and operated by couples.

Finally, some estimates say that up to 85% of new jobs in North America are created by small business, and couple-owned businesses make up the majority of that percentage.

## b. RATE OF SUCCESS

It is difficult to find statistics about the actual number of couple-owned and operated businesses in North America. Many are registered as home-based, some are registered only in the name of one spouse or partner, and others are part of a franchise listing not necessarily compiled by partnership profile. We do know, however, that at least 50% of all small businesses that start in any year will fail within that year. Since we know that a large number of these are run by couples, we can extrapolate that the same reasons for business failure would apply to couple-run businesses.

On average, couple entrepreneurs need at least two years to "get the bugs out" of their operations. They need to test their business plan against the market. If they are opening an office or a store, the logistics of opening, cash flow, marketing, production, and the other day-to-day mechanics of the business take time to learn. Couple-owned businesses that do not make it past the first two years fail for these reasons:

(a) They never developed a business plan that included their individual hopes, needs, and goals for the business.

(b) They assumed that because they cared about each other, no other planning was needed to make the business succeed.

(c) They allowed their personal conflicts to go unresolved and let them spill over into the business, creating confusion and indecision.

(d) They could not share power, authority, or decision-making.

(e) They could not allow each other to make mistakes and learn from those mistakes.

(f) They had incompatible goals for the business or for the relationship.

Couples who have successfully operated their business together have these characteristics in common:

(a) They view the business and the relationship as a joint responsibility, win or fail.

(b) They had shared values about work, people, money, and success. More important, they clearly knew that they shared these values. No assumptions were made.

(c) They clearly outlined individual responsibilities and tasks, including what roles their children and other family members would play.

(d) They had strategies for resolving conflicts.

(e) They set aside regular time for relaxation and play, where no business was allowed.

Interviews with successful couples show that those who received outside help and advice became successful more quickly than those who did not, and their businesses flourished more consistently. This outside advice came from business advisers, counselors, bankers, other entrepreneurs, and friends. It seems that this external help allows couples to get much needed objectivity, and to shorten the learning curve required in running a business.

The most successful couples took advantage of business training programs, government-sponsored loans and subsidies, business counseling, retreats, and workshops. Those who were not successful viewed these programs as interruptions, annoyances, too expensive, or too "touchy-feely." They felt they had the expertise and drive to make it on their own, but sadly, many of them were not successful, either in their business or their relationship.

When we asked couples what they found to be satisfying about running a business together, they were vocal and united in their responses. Although working and living so closely together tested their resources, all of them said that they had grown personally and professionally in ways that would not have been available to them in the corporate work world. If there were burdens, they could be shared. No longer did one spouse have to appear sympathetic to a workplace challenge the other was describing. Each person knew that the other was completely familiar with the challenge and was equally committed to a positive outcome. Travel, household chores, family responsibilities, bank loans, cash flow projections, school meetings — no matter what the task, partners had a new appreciation for what was required to get the job done.

### In it together

At the end of the day, Shannon and Jack are sitting on the floor in the den, surrounded by papers. Their five-year-old daughter has been asleep for two hours, and their teenage son is doing his homework in his bedroom.

Shannon and Jack are preparing a presentation for the bank tomorrow because they want a small business loan to expand their inventory by three new products. They have been in business together for 18 months, after leaving careers that had become stagnant and frustrating. They wholesale a line of incentive gift ideas, and up to now have used their savings and credit cards to finance their business. They have decided that Jack will handle the presentation and Shannon will answer the detailed questions they expect from the banker, since that is her area of expertise.

Even though it is late at night, they are excited by the opportunity the new inventory will present and they know they will work on the presentation until it is perfect. If they get this loan, they will have to hire someone to help them, and this is the first real expansion they will face. Their dream is underway, and they are in it together.

# 2

## ARE YOU READY TO RUN A BUSINESS TOGETHER?

By now the two of you have probably had many lengthy discussions about starting and running a business together. You have probably decided what type of business you will run and may have even made some strategies for running your new company. You have the makings of a solid business plan, and you have lined up the funds and budgets needed to make your business work. Both of you are excited about getting the business going and seeing your dream turn into reality. Because of your discussions, you both realize that there will be times when the two of you will disagree on business decisions, but you are confident that your personal relationship and communication skills can resolve any problems.

Too many couples assume that a caring relationship and trust in one another on a personal level will translate into the ideal business partnership. You may agree on the type of business you want to operate, but do you share all of the same goals? How many hours are you each willing to work? How long will you give the business to return a livable income? Do you feel the same way about things?

Before you go any further with your business planning, you need to take the time to make sure that working together will work out. The long-term success of your business and of your "partnership" depends on your ability as a couple to create and run a business that satisfies each of your needs for income, workload, responsibility, and job satisfaction.

Many couples find that running a business together challenges their trust in one another and forces them to deal with many uncomfortable issues. Frequently, the progress of your business depends upon your ability to work out differences quickly and smoothly. While the process of working together is challenging, your reward is a relationship that matures and strengthens much faster than if you did not work together.

Worksheet #1 at the end of this chapter, the Business Readiness Inventory, is a tool for you to use to identify specific areas where you as a couple are strong, and areas where you may need to spend time in improving your skills. It is important that each partner complete all the sections on his or her own, separately and privately. This will allow for careful consideration of the questions and more accurate responses. Once each of you has completed Worksheet #1, compare and discuss your answers. You may choose to trade your completed worksheets and read your partner's answers privately, before discussing them.

The remainder of this chapter provides you with explanations, examples, and suggestions regarding each section of Worksheet #1.

## a. SECTION 1: PERSONALLY SPEAKING

This first section focuses on how each of you, as partners in a relationship, value and invest in your relationship. It is important that you invest as much time and energy into building and protecting your relationship as you do in building and developing the business. Having a strong personal relationship is vital to any couple-run business. The stresses and strains of operating the business constantly put pressure on your relationship and challenge your trust in each other. The success of your business is based for the most part on how effectively and efficiently the management team works together. This working relationship is built on a clear understanding of each other's needs and expectations, both in and out of the business.

7

## Making time

Joan and Hank really enjoyed spending time together and were certain that running a business together would allow them to spend even more time with each other. When they compared their results from Section 1 of Worksheet #1, Hank was surprised to learn that Joan felt that their relationship was faltering. "All we ever talk about any more is the business; it's running our lives," says Joan. "We never seem to spend any time just being together as a couple any more." Hank and Joan decided to dedicate private time together by making specific "appointments" where they would only speak about things that did not involve the business. This approach ensured that they would be able to maintain a personal relationship that could coexist with the business.

Couples who work well together have made very clear decisions about how to protect and nurture their relationship and have translated this commitment into formal actions, such as scheduling private non-business time together.

If either of you scored less than 24 in Section 1, or if any of your answers were more than one point apart, then the two of you need to solidify your relationship. One of the most effective actions is to schedule regular time together and focus on each other, not business issues. Booking time together is a powerful action to take, as it clearly shows that you are investing in your relationship and that your relationship is important.

Use the questions in this section to lead your discussion. As you discuss each question, you will also be discovering each other's needs for privacy, credit, and family involvement. This process will be vital to the success of your business, as it recognizes the importance of a strong personal relationship on the management of a new business.

## b. SECTION 2: COMMUNICATION AND CONFLICT RESOLUTION

Section 2 deals with how well you as a couple operate and make decisions when facing challenging and stressful situations. Most couple-run businesses operate smoothly under conditions that are predictable, stable, and routine. However, in the world of business ownership, it can take years before your business will be a stable one with no surprises and only a few challenging situations. Learning to expect and even plan for difficult situations can help minimize stress and build the confidence of the management team.

How do each of you recognize and deal with stress? Are your approaches similar or very different? Complete Section 2 carefully, taking time to think through each answer. Each of you should complete this section privately, without time limits or pressures.

### Trouble signs

Mark and Susan operate a small bakery with eight employees. The bakery operates 20 hours a day, six days a week. Mark is responsible for the baking and Susan is in charge of the employees, administration, and sales. Although they both knew that bakeries need to start at 4:00 a.m. to ensure that the products are on the shelves by opening time, neither of them had considered the toll that such long hours would take on their health and relationship.

Susan realized how far apart they had become when she compared her answers in Section 2 of Worksheet #1 to Mark's. "We never have any time to talk any more, and when we do it's usually at the end of the day when we are both exhausted. Trying to deal with problems when we are both tired usually ends up in a fight and then we still have to go home together."

Mark was surprised to learn that Susan felt that they did not deal well with problems. "Susan always overreacts to problems, making mountains out of mole hills. She's got the easy job anyway, working 9:00 to 5:00 with staff to help her. The last thing I want to do at the end of the day is deal with problems that she should be able to handle herself."

In this example, the worksheet has specifically identified a problem area for Mark and Susan. Clearly, Susan expects to be able to rely on her partner to discuss business problems, not only to develop solutions together but also to share the experience with him. Mark, on the other hand wants only to focus on his "job" of baking and does not see himself involved in the other aspects of the business.

This issue is very common for couples in businesses together, as it is a combination of different expectations, poor conflict resolution skills, and fatigue. The challenge now is for Mark and Susan to decide on a course of action regarding this problem. Following are just a few suggestions for actions that Mark and Susan could try:

(a) Book time throughout the normal work day to have a management meeting to discuss problems. This would also keep Mark up-to-date on all the facets of the business.

(b) Make an agreement that clearly delegates complete authority of certain decision areas to Susan so Mark's input on specific areas would no longer be required.

(c) Involve staff more in problem solving. This action will only work if the problems can be solved by staff, and certainly will not work if any of the problems are being caused by staff members.

(d) Do nothing and maintain the pattern that already exists. This is a very common approach to conflict. While this approach does not solve anything, it at least does not require either partner to change his or her expectations.

As you can see, this section deals primarily with how well you as a couple operate under stress and deal with negative situations. Dealing with stress and solving conflicts are essential management skills. These skills are even more important when the management team faces business, personal, and interpersonal stresses together. The information in chapter 5 will help you develop your conflict resolution skills further.

## c. SECTION 3: BUSINESS PARTICIPATION

Section 3 of Worksheet #1 deals with the business and the management style that each of you brings to your responsibilities. It will give you a clear indication of the expectations that each of you have for each other's workload and motivations.

### Learning each other's style

Lynne and John operate a business sales training company. Lynne is primarily involved with developing and presenting the sales seminars as well as virtually all of the aspects involved with getting and keeping customers. John handles the office support and administration and is primarily responsible for ensuring that the presentations are organized and on budget.

After completing Section 3, Lynne was surprised to learn that although John felt that he understood Lynne's motivations for working, he did not feel that Lynne understood his reasons for working. He described Lynne's motivations as striving for the excitement and recognition that comes with delivering successful presentations and having a roomful of customers seek her advice. It was obvious that Lynne was always looking for improvement, and if that meant constantly changing and fine-tuning a presentation, then she would go ahead and make the changes.

"You're right John, that's what I love. I'm always looking for ways to change and improve. It's a challenge and I'm up for it. But isn't it what you love too?" Lynne asked.

John pointed out that while he was always happy for her when a presentation went well, he was more interested in making the overall running of the business more precise and consistent. "I don't want this business to excite me. I just want it to provide us with a profit level and personal income that is predictable and steady," he said.

Lynne and John have now realized how different their reasons for working are and that they each measure success differently. They reviewed their business objectives to make sure that their target goals would not conflict with John's need for consistency and Lynne's need for change.

Section 3 should have you both looking at your reasons for wanting to work together and your expectations for the direction that the business will take. Now is the time to talk about the mission of your company and develop a shared business vision.

## d. SECTION 4: WHEN ONLY ONE OF YOU WORKS AT THE BUSINESS (BUT THE OTHER MAY JOIN)

This final section is designed for couples who only have one partner involved in the business, but there is a possibility that the second partner will also become involved. This is an especially important section to complete because this is the most common way that couples end up running a business together. Sometimes the other partner has made a clear commitment to join the company, but most often, life partners have no initial desire to join the business, but occasionally "help out." Eventually, the life partner ends up being responsible for many segments of the company on a full-time basis.

### More than a helper

Pat operates a small construction firm specializing in stucco and gyp roc installation. Each year the business has grown, adding customers, equipment, and employees. Pat works an average of 14 hours per day and is running as fast as he can to keep up with the physical labor as well as the administrative side of the business. When he is not working at the business, he is either talking about it, thinking about it, or sleeping.

Betty finds that one way to spend more time with Pat is to take care of some of the administrative work after she comes home from her job and before Pat comes in from the construction work. This way, with some of the paperwork caught up, they can spend time together in the evenings. Betty's "help" quickly turns into a second job because she soon takes on the additional tasks of bookkeeping, invoicing, paying bills, meeting with the accountant on her lunch hour, completing payroll information, and submitting the appropriate taxes and remittances. Eventually Betty cannot keep up with the workload on a part-time basis, and the business clearly needs her full time. Pat and Betty decide that the time has come for Betty to join the business.

Will Betty join as a co-member of the management team, or is she a junior clerk? Pat's answers to Section 4 will determine how ready he is to accept Betty into the company, and how willing he is to accept her advice and decisions. Too often couples "end up" in business together, while one partner still feels as though the business is his or hers alone. This approach is successful only if both partners agree to it before they join forces.

In this situation, Pat and Betty decided that Betty would join the company initially in the formal capacity of administrative manager, and as she became more familiar with operations and revenue, her responsibilities would grow into that of a managing partner. To accomplish this transition, they developed a written job description for Betty that detailed what her responsibilities would be, what she is expected to complete, and the amount of time required. The job description also had a salary value attached, so that even though Betty may not actually take a paycheck (for tax or lack of cash flow reasons), her job would have an expressed value that Pat would have to acknowledge. This action satisfies a number of important issues:

(a) A job description ensures that jobs get done by the right person with no overlap and clearly defines Betty's role.

(b) A salary value forces both partners to realize the value of Betty's assistance, with the result that both partners take Betty's work more seriously.

(c) Since the amount and scope of Betty's duties is clearly set out, the company will be able to determine whether and when to hire another administrative employee.

(d) As the job matures and Betty's activities widen, the job description could also be used as an indicator of when Betty could move into more of a management role.

This approach is very successful as it ensures that both members of the couple are clear as to what their roles are, and it identifies what type of business relationship they share, whether that of co-partners, or owner and employee, or owner and adviser.

In this section, your scores will reflect how often you discuss the business as well as identify whether your discussions have tended to center on problems, solutions, or successes that the business faces. The "external" partner will be accepted into the company faster if your discussions have been a blend of these points or have involved the external partner in developing solutions. Partners who solve problems are always treated with more respect that those who are only available to listen to either problems or successes.

# WORKSHEET #1
## BUSINESS READINESS INVENTORY

For each statement, think how strongly you agree/disagree. Answer every question in every section. Have your partner repeat the process, **but wait until he or she has completed the assessment** before you compare your answers. Put your answers on separate sheets so you won't influence each other. The differences in your answers indicate the areas you need to work on together. You may find it easier to complete this worksheet by each of you answering and discussing one section at a time, rather than the entire worksheet at once.

Scores: **3** = Strongly agree   **1** = Disagree somewhat
**2** = Agree somewhat   **0** = Strongly disagree

### Section 1: Personally speaking

1. We always maintain a sense of humor when things go wrong. _____

2. We do not blame each other when things go wrong. _____

3. We take time to celebrate each other's successes. _____

4. We join forces against the outside world. "United We Stand" is our motto. _____

5. If the limelight falls on my partner, I view that positively and not enviously or disrespectfully. _____

6. We have a regular time scheduled that we spend relaxing in non-business activities, as a couple together. _____

7. We have agreed on a division of domestic and family/child care responsibilities that we are both comfortable with. _____

8. Our needs for work and personal time are compatible. _____

9. We never talk about work at home, unless it is a crisis. _____

10. We both invest as much time into building our relationship as we do our careers. _____

11. We can always rely on each other to be supportive of each other. _____

**Now add up your score for this section:** _____

### Section 2: Communication and conflict resolution

1. Our relationship has been tested sufficiently so we know how we function as a couple under stress. _____

2. We formally meet several times a year to talk about how things are going. _____

3. We talk problems out when they arise, not letting them fester. _____

4. We work well on projects we have undertaken together. _____

5. We openly express differences of opinion without consequence. _____

6. We are able to resolve all our major conflicts and differences to a mutual agreement. _____

7. We have a clear process for making decisions and sharing power. _____

8. We can disagree without taking it personally or attacking each other personally. _____

9. We are able to focus on the future and not dwell on past conflicts. _____

10. We separate our work relationship from home. _____

11. My work is not any more important than my spouse's. _____

**Now add up your score for this section:** _____

**Section 3 : Business participation**

1. We evaluate clearly and objectively our performance in the business. _____

2. We recognize each person's contribution as equally important and valuable. _____

3. We have clear responsibilities and roles. _____

4. We are both willing to pitch in and do tasks we do not like to do. _____

5. We have complementary skills/talents. _____

6. We have a written business plan that is evaluated and updated regularly. _____

7. My spouse clearly understands my motivations and goals for working. _____

8. I clearly understand my spouse's motivations and goals for working. _____

9. We have planned for each of us to grow and change beyond our present responsibilities. _____

10. We share our dreams and vision of the future and know what each other wants. _____

11. We have agreed on a division of responsibilities and know who will be "boss" of what. _____

**Now add up your score for this section:** _____

**Section 4: When only one of you works at the business**

1. My spouse never has questions/comments/ suggestions about my business that I feel are intrusive or not his or her concern. _____

2. My spouse always understands/cares what I feel about my business. _____

3. My spouse never takes credit for successes that I am responsible for. _____

4. My spouse is always willing to talk with me about the business. _____

5. I am happy to talk to my spouse about the business anytime he or she wants to. _____

6. Most of the time, my spouse has questions/comments/suggestions about my business that are really valuable to me. _____

7. I always feel that I can talk to my spouse about the business. _____

8. I want to involve my spouse more in the business. _____

9. I consider my spouse to be a valuable "consultant" to the business. _____

10. I can always count on my spouse to understand and accept those times when the business takes precedence over everything else. _____

11. We always keep our commitments to each other. _____

**Now add up your score for this section:** _____

**About your score**

The highest score attainable for each section is 33. A score of 33 indicates a solid support base and strong communication skills. A score of 25 or higher indicates that there are some areas that you and your spouse need to work on to improve your focus at work and strengthen your relationship. Scores between 18 to 24 indicate many areas to work on as well as some areas of disagreement. Scores of 18 and lower indicate problems that are negatively affecting your profits and stress levels; a high priority should be placed on improving skills in these areas.

# 3

## BUILDING A SUCCESSFUL BUSINESS

As your business ages and progresses, it changes and develops with the experience of the management team and your knowledge of your market. As your business matures and becomes profitable, it also becomes more stable.

By no means is progress guaranteed. Many businesses never move out of the development stage. The owners spend most of their time handling one crisis after another, reacting to what is happening to their business, instead of planning and following detailed strategies.

It is vital that the business progress to the next stage. Staying too long in any stage usually results in "burn out" for the owners and the eventual demise or sale of the company.

## a. FACTORS THAT AFFECT PROGRESS

### Burning out

Laurie and Rees operate a young but successful printing company. They are both past professionals in the printing industry and have over 30 years of experience between them. They started their own printing business six years ago, certain that with their combination of skills, contacts, and experience their business would be a success in no time. They sketched out a business plan, divided up their responsibilities, and opened their doors.

For the first two years everything went according to plan. They enjoyed a steady increase in customers and had just hired their first two employees. They worked long hours, with Laurie contacting and selling to customers and

19

Rees operating the presses and managing the staff. With the increased revenue came an increase in profits, but not nearly at the levels that they had planned on. So they worked harder, putting in longer hours and trying for more business.

In addition to their workload, they found that frequent changes in technology forced them to upgrade their two-year-old equipment into newer, faster, and more expensive machines. To reduce their expenses, they laid off one employee and split the additional workload between them. This continued for another three years, with revenues staying ahead of expenses, but not enough for them to take a livable wage and hire more staff to take over some of the workload.

"It feels as though this business is not progressing past the growth stage," Laurie said. "It always feels as though we go three steps forward and two back, and I'm getting tired of working so hard for such little result." Rees pointed out that although most of the business was going according to plan, "it's the same plan we had for the first two years. We never thought that we would still be working this hard after five years."

Ultimately Laurie and Rees will have to make a tough decision: to sell or close the business before it wears them out, or to make some radical changes to the way they operate so that they can progress to the next stage and beyond. They wrongly assumed that the business would progress largely on the basis of their past experience and the amount of effort that they put in. They did not examine the possibility that progress also depends on how closely the plan fits the ever-changing nature of their industry. Laurie and Rees could not reach the level of profits where they could hire employees to take over daily tasks. If they are ever going to lead the company, and not just work for it, they need to have other staff carry on the day-to-day operation.

If your business can't progress and grow, there is a danger that you and your partner will burn out and have to give up. There are several factors that affect progress:

(a) The ability of the management team to keep their vision of what this business will eventually look like

(b) How well the management team compares actual results and strategies with planned results and strategies

(c) The ability of the management team to analyze the results of decisions they have made: how well risk was balanced with reward

(d) The frequency and magnitude of mistakes made

(e) How well the business masters each stage of development before moving on to the next stage

(f) How the management team learns and applies different styles to each stage of development

If your business is to succeed, there are definite stages of development that you must attain (see Sample #1). Each calls for a different management style. Look at the stages as stepping stones toward building a strong and profitable company, where each of you gets to see your dreams of success realized. Each stage can be clearly identified by measuring areas such as systems, management style, and profit consistency.

## SAMPLE #1
## STAGES OF BUSINESS DEVELOPMENT

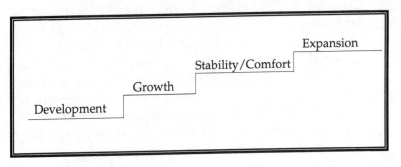

## b.  STAGE 1: DEVELOPMENT

This is where it all begins. You and your partner decide to start a business. You have many discussions about what it will be like when the business is successful. You are excited and full of energy. Everything about this stage is filled with anticipation.

This is the time for creation, for trial and error. At this stage you are not yet working as independent members of a management team, but are relying on each other to do every task and every job that needs doing. Your job tasks are not clearly defined because neither of you is certain about what will be needed next, and you both need and want to be able to do whatever it takes to make the business work!

You pour a lot of time and energy into the business, and you do see some results. The results are not quite the ones you anticipated, but they are close. Even though you expected to be very busy, you didn't anticipate quite this amount of work. You spend a lot of time running out of time.

Your management style at this stage needs to be very results-oriented and success-driven. Both partners need to be willing and able to take risks and make decisions quickly even in areas where you have little or no experience. This is the stage where most of your mistakes will be made and repaired, so get used to it.

### Style is everything

Christine and David started a fine art business specializing in supplying art to the corporate market through sales and rentals. Both Christine and David had sales experience and loved to deal with customers and revenue creation. They started their business by dividing up their contacts and determining what they would present to each customer. They kept their expenses low by borrowing the art from the artists and buying it only when they had a purchase order from a customer.

They each kept track of things by writing notes in their daytimers and having brief catch-up meetings.

They shared a style that enjoyed taking risks, meeting with people, and measuring their success based on how many sales they were creating. Neither liked to do paperwork as they both considered it to be unimportant and boring. "All that paperwork junk is stuff that should be done after the important work is completed," shared David. "Without sales we don't have a company."

When artists stopped allowing Christine and David to borrow art until their last bill was paid, the couple put it down to "Artists are so emotional, they just don't understand business." It wasn't until they received final notice from the tax office to pay all back remittances owing within five days or be prosecuted that David and Christine realized how the style that got them into business was likely to put them out of business.

"I never realized how my style of being a forward thinker and always looking for the next sale could actually harm our success," Christine said. "It wasn't until someone forced us to really finish with each piece of business, including the paperwork, that we had to make some changes."

Now David and Christine set aside time each week to catch up on their paperwork, and they have hired an accountant to help them stay on top of the administrative side of the business. Their change in style has helped them to repair any problems with art suppliers and ensures that they won't be surprised by any more tax notices.

Is your business stuck in the development stage? Look at Checklist #1. If the statements describe your business, you may want to review your situation and see how you can gain strength. Here are some aspects of your business you should give more attention to:

(a) Write a business plan and break it down into monthly and weekly activities.

(b) Build time into your weekly routine to review and revise progress and strategies against your business plan.

(c) Learn to learn fast. You do not have enough time to make any mistake twice.

(d) This is the time to build your reputation, so fix mistakes and fix them well.

(e) Learn from others. Surround yourself with a network of stronger, more mature businesses.

(f) Develop a "return on investment" approach to your business. Every dollar and hour you spend should give you some return greater than what you have put in.

(g) Develop good management habits now; you will need them every step of the way.

## c. STAGE 2: GROWTH

You are no longer reacting to what is happening to the business. Many of the expectations you had have happened as you anticipated. You are gaining market share, but not enough for competitors to respond. More of your tasks are repetitive now than in the development stage, although you still need to have very general skills and be able to adapt to a wide variety of demands. You have begun to identify which plans are working and which are not. You now see a definite return on investment, although it is not as high or as consistent as you had planned.

### Master of all trades

Steve and Helen operate a commercial janitorial service that offers cleaning services to schools and government buildings. Steve is primarily involved with making the

# CHECKLIST #1
## THE DEVELOPMENT STAGE

**Your business is in the development stage if —**

1. Sales and profits are not consistent, and may not be happening at all.

2. More money is going into the business than is coming out of it.

3. No repetitive systems or routines are in place. Everything in the business is being created on the run.

4. Papers pile up on your desk, not only because you don't have time to get to them, but also because you don't yet have a specific place or system for dealing with each piece of information.

5. Job tasks and responsibilities are not separated and assigned to separate individuals.

6. Outside expertise is not being utilized.

7. There is not enough time in the day to get everything done.

8. Management focus is on creating customers, products, and services.

9. Results are taking much longer to happen than anticipated.

sales presentations to customers, completing the quotes, and managing the cleaning crews. Helen runs the office and has little contact with customers.

Recently, near the end of a ski weekend, Steve took a bad fall and broke his leg. He will not be mobile for some time. In addition to being concerned for his injury and pain, Helen realized that Steve has an important sales presentation booked for Monday. "I knew I could have called the client and canceled, but I didn't think we'd get another chance at this account. And I didn't want Steve to feel any worse about his accident than he already did," said Helen. "I'd never made a sales pitch before, but I had to get over my fear and make the presentation so we would get the business. I did okay. I think that my fear translated itself into excitement; we got the account."

Being able to cover for each other in your business is an important skill, as it ensures that the business will have all of its needs met, even if a different person has to fill them occasionally. For your business to survive the growth stage, both members of your team have to be flexible in their jobs and be able to add new skills quickly. Growth demands further growth, with no room for the management team to stop and catch up.

Review Checklist #2 to see if your business has reached the growth stage.

If your business is going to move beyond the growth stage, you need to look at ways to make your operation more efficient. You may also need to consult with other entrepreneurs who have successfully navigated the growth stage. Here are some steps you can take:

(a) Delegate job tasks to the best person, not the one with the most time.

(b) Develop marketing systems that will help you react to the competition; they are about to notice you.

(c) Analyze products and services for their profitability, and drop those that don't give you a profit.

(d) Begin to have "specialist" job functions. Develop staff training plans and job descriptions for each specialist, even if some people are responsible for more than one job.

(e) Create a "board of advisers" from your network to keep you focused and committed to your plan.

# CHECKLIST #2
## THE GROWTH STAGE

---

**Your business is in the growth stage if —**

1. The business is consistently breaking even, and occasionally showing a small profit.
2. Systems and strategies are still being added everywhere.
3. Repeat customers are just starting to appear.
4. You now have a market or customer base that is contacting you.
5. Management focus is still largely on marketing although some staffing issues are now occurring.

---

## Creating an advisory board

Kelly and Bob run a small cafe that specializes in luscious desserts and cakes. They are located in a small strip mall and their lease runs out in five months. They have had many discussions about whether or not to stay in their present location or move to a new one.

"We've only been in business for three years. We decided to ask other people for their opinion, partly because we are so close to this business that we can't see the forest for the trees, and also because we wanted to make sure we were making the right decisions. An advisory board seemed like the right way to get the opinions of people we respected and trusted," said Bob.

Kelly and Bob invited their accountant, Bob's father, two long-time customers, and their banker to meet with them quarterly and give them advice. "We chose this group of people because we wanted to balance the input between business and customers, and because each of them really want to see us succeed," Kelly points out. "Besides, they really helped us with the lease decision. Our banker and accountant reviewed the lease from a numbers perspective, while our customers and Bob's father saw the decision from the viewpoint of our customers. Now we are moving to a better location beside a movie theater and inviting all of our present customers to a grand opening event. Without our advisory board, we never would have considered our new location and we would not have thought of how to keep our existing customers. An extra benefit is that our banker and accountant now understand us better. We are learning skills from them as well as the rest of the advisory board."

Advisory boards can be formed from your network of suppliers, customers, and peers. Make sure to choose people who are committed to your success and will tell you their opinion even if you won't agree with it. Board members are usually unpaid, because payment could involve liability, but they should be rewarded for their involvement through gifts or invitations to dinner, etc.

## d. STAGE 3: COMFORT

This is the stage that finally shows you the results that you have been waiting for. Although you are doing many of the same activities that you were in your growth stage, this is where almost everything you do gives you a return on investment. You no longer have to create sales as much as add to each sale. A large part of your customer base is now repeat buyers and those referred by existing clients. Your staff know their jobs, and most work independently from one another. More of your day is spent dealing with human resources and planning the next quarter than in dealing with the daily sales and yesterday's paperwork.

While in the earlier stages you managed massive change and strove for consistency, in this stage you should try to minimize change and build consistency. In the comfort stage there is very little need for creative energy or immediate reactions to issues because most of the results are exactly as anticipated. For many business owners, this is the stage that gives you the "breather" that you so desperately needed in development and growth, but were too busy to get. The comfort stage is also the place where many business owners reevaluate just where they want their company to go, and how hard they are willing to continue to work to get it there.

### Learning to let go — just a little

Lorna and Dave's pet store has reached the comfort and stability stage. They finally have their evenings back and the occasional weekend, something that they have not allowed for the first six years of operation. Lorna finds herself busy making social plans to reconnect with all of their friends who had so patiently waited for them to become available again.

On the evening of their first dinner party in years, Dave tells Lorna that he has got to return to the shop to clean up the cages, because the employee in charge of those tasks has called in sick. Dave will be gone at least three hours, and Lorna knows he has a habit of always finding more work to do whenever he is in the shop. Lorna says, "We have other staff who can do that job Dave, and we set aside tonight to be with our friends. I'm really beginning to resent how you always put the business first, even when it doesn't need you."

Dave clearly has not trained himself to let the business run itself, which is exactly the payoff of reaching the comfort stage. This problem is common with entrepreneurs because they work so hard and for so long building and protecting their business that they don't know how to sit back and let the business run itself for a time while they recharge their batteries. Part of the solution is to learn to recognize the signs that indicate that your business has reached the comfort stage. The other part of the solution lies with the co-owners: take time out to reestablish your connections with the rest of your life. Then you can get excited again about owning a business.

**Plans can change**

Charlie and Sheila run a successful consulting business, servicing the owners of retail stores. When they started the business, they planned to let it grow to the stage where they could each run a separate division of the company, as well as take two weeks vacation every three months. The business followed their plans exactly until one day Charlie burst into Sheila's office: "Great news! I've just signed a deal with a major national retailer who wants us to consult with each of their 58 stores all across this country! We could even set up offices in some of the cities and go after some more national retailers. Finally our company is really on its way!"

Sheila congratulated Charlie on the deal, but reminded him that this plan wasn't what they agreed to do with their growth. "We planned on running one large operation that would allow us to take more time off for vacation. I think that we should re-think this and see if we can find a way to get out of the deal." Charlie and Sheila spent many hours looking at the advantages and disadvantages that this opportunity presented. Eventually it became clear that they no longer shared the same vision for their company. Charlie just couldn't pass up "the deal of a lifetime," and Sheila did not want to put more time and energy into growing a business that demanded a lot of travel and left very little personal time.

They decided to compromise, with Sheila managing the small original company and Charlie traveling and setting up offices nationwide. With drastically reduced time together, and the knowledge that they no longer shared a dream, their personal relationship deteriorated and they divorced. As well, their business partnership ended.

Has your company grown to the point where you should be able to sit back and enjoy some of the things you used to do together before you started your business? Are you content with this level of success? See Checklist #3 for the signs that indicate that you are experiencing the comfort stage.

### CHECKLIST #3
### THE COMFORT STAGE

**Your business is in the comfort stage if —**

1. Revenue and profit is consistent and stable.

2. Most of the job tasks are routine and repetitive.

3. Systems are in place to handle all job tasks and information needs.

4. Outside experts are used in special areas such as legal and financial management.

5. The people involved have responsibilities and functions that are independent of each other.

6. The business operates by following business plan strategies that are based on ensuring a consistent return on investment.

7. Management focus is now on human resources, placing the right people in the right jobs.

8. Operations and policy manuals are followed consistently by every member of the organization.

9. New members each have a job position training and orientation plan.

At this stage, you should review your plan for your business once again. If you want to continue in this profitable, stable stage, you should do the following:

(a) Acquire management skills to analyze each area of the company: financial, human resources, marketing, and operations

(b) Compare the achievements of the company to the business plan

(c) Create new products and services only if the company really needs them

(d) Ensure that your entire team functions well together and that no one is indispensable

(e) Spend time researching and developing the next actions of your company

## e. STAGE 4: EXPANSION

Finally — the stage you've been striving for! At this stage, your company is making a consistent profit that is much higher than during the comfort stage. In the expansion stage you are again adding systems and people to your company, but now you are repeating only your successes, not your mistakes. The expansion stage feels a lot like the growth stage, with plenty of changes and creative energy. The biggest difference between expansion and growth is that expansion activities are planned successes based on a proven track record, while growth is the stage where success was a result of trial and error.

The company is now run by a team of experts, each a specialist in his or her area of responsibility. Your management style now needs to be that of a team coordinator and visionary, capable of leading the company into the arena of fast-paced growth and high investment return. See Checklist #4 to determine if your business is already in, or is ready to enter, the expansion stage.

# CHECKLIST #4
## THE EXPANSION STAGE

**Your business is in the expansion stage if —**

1. You have consistent profits of greater than 20% per year.
2. Your revenues come from diversified markets or client bases.
3. Effective and efficient systems are in place throughout the company.
4. Each job is well-defined and completed by specialists.
5. Management focus is on the expansion of company profits through diversification of market or location.
6. Management consists of a team of experts for each department.

## Trusting the team

Sharon and Jeff's muffler business was expanding fast. They had recently decided to franchise their business, and with the help of a consultant, had put together a team that would lead their company into the world of expanding through franchising. "I didn't know the members of our new team very well, since I had never worked with any of them and was relying on the advice of our franchise consultant. It sure was an uncomfortable feeling, having these strangers making decisions that would affect Sharon's and my future," Jeff said. "But we knew they could help us if we let them."

Jeff and Sharon had to learn to be part of a team and not make decisions or take actions that were not part of the agreed-upon plan. "The hardest part of the expansion was having to ask for and take the advice of our new 'inside experts,' even if what they wanted to do was different from how we wanted to do it," Sharon said. "In the past, only Jeff and I had to come to agreement. Now there are six of us and it takes much longer to reach consensus."

The expansion was successful and the management team continues to lead the company into new markets.

The expansion stage does risk the stability you have gained in your business so far. If you are determined to forge ahead, keep in mind the following:

(a) Learn to take risks again, but make sure your risk analysis is strong.

(b) Develop a plan for expansion and stick to it.

(c) Ensure that the expansion complements and builds on the strengths of the existing company.

(d) Match the rate of expansion to the demands of the market and the talents of your team.

(e) Become a coach and not a boss.

(f) Listen to and trust your team. Give them more authority.

### Important — but not irreplaceable

"'Nobody can do the job as well as I can,' is the way I used to think about our business," explains Serge. "Now I'm finding that my wife and I have done such a good job training our staff, that quite often they can do it faster and better than we can. Many times the most we have to do is let the staff know that what they do is important to us and that they don't have to be perfect either. Our staff now look to us as coaches instead of star players. It takes a while to get used to not being indispensable, but it can also be quite freeing."

René, Serge's wife and business partner adds: "The upside of having your employees running the daily operations of the business is that you are no longer bogged down with the mundane details. But the upside has a downside in that sometimes I feel very disjointed and out of touch with how the 'real life' part of the business is doing. Sometimes I have to go back onto the shop floor for an afternoon, just to get my feelers back."

Learning when to let go is an important skill for business owners. Too often the expansion of the business is stalled because the owners will not let others take over some of the aspects of operating the company. When the owners step back from the daily operations, they can then focus on leading the company through the expansion stage to real growth and wealth.

# 4

## DEFINING ROLES AND RESPONSIBILITIES

### a. DECIDING WHO DOES WHAT

It is rare for one person to have all the skills required to run a successful business. Couples choose to go into business together to take advantage of complementary or very opposite skills, but seldom are their skills exactly the same. Successful businesses have systems and procedures that are efficient, clear, and reliable. People in the business know what their jobs are and how to accomplish them.

One of the most common sources of conflict in a couple-operated business is role confusion. Each person needs to have clear, defined, separate roles that allow full use of individual skills. Division of labor in a company can happen in several of the following ways. Whichever way you choose, it is important that you formally divide the tasks it takes to run your business and your household.

With your partner, brainstorm a complete list of all the tasks it takes to run your business and your household. Use a couple of pieces of flip chart paper and tape the sheets to the wall. Label one sheet "Household" and the other one "Business." Unless your private-life responsibilities are taken care of, you won't be able to give full attention to your business.

Fill up both sheets with every task you can think of. Then, on a separate piece of paper, write down those tasks for which you want to be responsible. This list should initially comprise those tasks that really excite you, that you are fully self-motivated to do. Include all the household tasks that you really enjoy.

You and your partner should now compare lists. Cross the tasks from your lists off the master lists on the flip chart pages. What tasks are left over? Are there things you both want to do? Are there things you both want to avoid? Discuss how the remaining tasks could be handled. Remember, you can ask someone else to do some of the things you both don't want to do.

Another option that couples may choose is to divide tasks so that each can learn skills or acquire knowledge in a new area. You may have always wanted to learn to cook, and this may be the perfect opportunity. Tell your spouse what it is you would like to learn, and build a plan for learning the skills as quickly as you can.

It is normal for people to want to claim the things they do well. In a successful business, each partner must respect the other's areas of expertise and focus on performing his or her own tasks well. No matter which method is used, the most important thing is that everyone in the business is clear about what his or her jobs are and what is required to make the business a success.

The most common business tool for clarifying roles and responsibilities is the job description. In business, job descriptions typically clarify the tasks that need to be performed, and group the tasks into larger topic areas. For example, buying advertising and writing weekly newspaper ads might fall under the larger heading of marketing. Job descriptions also state the quality standards that must be met. In most large businesses, job descriptions form the basis for the following:

(a) Recruiting: Job descriptions are used in writing effective recruiting advertisements.

(b) Interviewing and selection: Clear job descriptions form the basis for behavioral interview questions. Job descriptions should be given to applicants at an interview so they know exactly what the job involves.

(c) Orientation and training: Job descriptions provide the framework for training employees to do the job well. Although you may have hired someone because he or she met your basic criteria, that person still needs to know the specifics of doing the job for you in your company. Job descriptions list the tasks and responsibilities in the position, and you can check the employee's knowledge and performance against the requirements of the job.

(d) Performance evaluation: Job descriptions help employees understand the standards of performance and any improvement required. When performance is compared against the job description, you are sure to be objective and to comment only on performance, not personality.

(e) Promotions/transfers: When there are rewards to be given out, you will want to make sure they are given to the top performers. Before you promote an employee, you can analyze his or her current skills and abilities based on the job description and compare them to the new skills required for the new job. This eliminates the risk of promoting someone above his or her level of competence.

Job descriptions play an important role in clarifying performance standards in any business. They are especially critical to the couple-owned business because, as we have already said, role confusion is a key source of conflict. For example, if you believe you are in charge of marketing and your partner buys some advertising without consultation, you might feel that your territory has been invaded or that your partner does not trust your ability to do your job. On the other hand, if you have not defined each person's area of responsibility, there is a strong possibility that certain tasks will fall through the cracks and be forgotten until a crisis pops up.

## b.  WRITE JOB DESCRIPTIONS FOR EACH OTHER

Writing job descriptions for each other is a two-step process. First, using Worksheet #2, or a separate piece of paper, write down the tasks that you identified as your specialty. Group them into categories (e.g., inventory control, marketing, child care, production, etc.). Identify any strengths that you believe are not being used and think of tasks or categories to which those strengths could be applied.

The second step is to use Worksheet #3 and do the same thing with your partner's list. When you have completed both steps, get together and analyze the results. Do you have categories that have overlapping tasks? How can you more clearly define who is responsible for them?

### Dividing up the dirty work

Mark and Lorna own a small bagel bakery and restaurant. Sample #2 shows how they defined all the tasks necessary to run their business and their home. Sample #3 shows which tasks they chose to do.

Mark and Lorna now face the challenge of deciding what to do about the tasks neither one of them chose, since they are necessary to the success of the business and the family relationship. They also need to decide what to do about the tasks that they both want to do.

Mark and Lorna realized that they both wanted to do the advertising, and they both wanted to arrange their home insurance. Neither of them enjoyed early mornings, so taking the kids to school was not attractive. They both felt that school meetings ate up precious evening time. At the end of their discussion, they agreed to have a cleaning service clean both the house and the store.

## WORKSHEET #2
## DEFINE YOUR JOB

1. What are the functions or divisions of the company for which you are responsible?

_____

_____

_____

_____

_____

_____

_____

_____

_____

_____

2. What are your strengths and how do you think the company could make better use of them?

_____

_____

_____

_____

_____

_____

_____

_____

_____

_____

## WORKSHEET #3
## DEFINE YOUR PARTNER'S JOB

1. What do you think your partner is responsible for in the company? Are there any areas you feel you would like to take over?

_____

_____

_____

_____

_____

_____

_____

_____

2. Share your lists and discuss areas of confusion or overlap. Are there any tasks or functions for which you both feel responsible? How can your roles be clarified?

_____

_____

_____

_____

_____

_____

_____

_____

They would each take the children to school on alternate weeks.

As they got their business underway, new tasks came up. For each new task, Mark and Lorna met to discuss their skills and willingness around that task. This way, they could see how the company was growing and changing, and their meetings prevented them from doing things at random with no consideration for the time it would take to carry out new duties and tasks.

For entrepreneurs, work expands to fill the time available. You may find yourself volunteering to take on tasks and functions until you suddenly run out of time for family, friends, and each other. A job description helps you decide what you take on and what you delegate. Being able to successfully portion time for the business and for your relationship ultimately means success for both.

When each partner in a company feels powerful and in control of a defined area of responsibility, it is easier to ask for help when you are uncertain how to proceed. You will also find it easier to give credit to your partner if you feel you have areas that you feel you have expertise. There may be some areas of the business in which your skills overlap, and even in these areas you need to decide who is accountable for results.

Clear job descriptions for the founding couple also ensure that employees cannot play one of you against the other. If employees know that only one of you will approve raises or vacation time or hiring decisions, they will feel secure and confident that decisions are final when they are made. If they know that there is a likelihood that one partner will countermand the other's decisions, confusion and manipulation will result, and the business will slide into chaos.

Every job in the company should have a clear job description. It is a good idea to allow employees to participate in writing their own job descriptions. Ask them to list the tasks

## TASKS FOR BUSINESS AND HOME

| Business | Household |
|---|---|
| Sales | Laundry |
| Advertising | Meals |
| Buying supplies | Taking the kids to school |
| Arrange financing | School meetings |
| Design logo | House cleaning |
| Negotiate lease | Supervising homework |
| Build marketing plan | Sports activities |
| Do direct mail campaign | Vacations |
| Paint the store | Car maintenance |
| Buy a computer | Home insurance |
| Equipment maintenance | Staying with sick kids |
| Cleaning the store | Birthday parties |
| Serve customers | Banking |
| Bake the bagels | |
| Invent new fillings | |

## SAMPLE #3
## PREFERRED TASKS

| "Mark's choices" | "Lorna's choices" |
|---|---|
| Sales | Design logo |
| Sports activities | Meals |
| Advertising | Supervising homework |
| Buying supplies | Vacations |
| Arrange financing | Home insurance |
| Negotiate lease | Staying with sick kids |
| Build marketing plan | Birthday parties |
| Paint the store | Serve customers |
| Buy a computer | Do direct mail campaign |
| Equipment maintenance | Invent new fillings |
| Bake the bagels | Advertising |
| Car maintenance | Banking |
| Home insurance | |

### "Tasks neither chose"
Cleaning the store
School meetings
Taking the kids to school
House cleaning
Laundry

or functions for which they are responsible. You and your partner should do the same for each job. It will quickly become clear where there are any areas of misunderstanding or role confusion. Sample #4 gives a guide to the minimum amount of information that should be in each person's job description.

### Knowing what you want

Eric and Marie run a women's retail clothing store. They have been working together for almost three years, and they are now seeking counseling for their troubled relationship. It seems that the business is successful on the surface, but neither one of them is happy. Eric continually finds fault with Marie's bookkeeping. In his disapproval, he often takes charge of making bank deposits because he feels that she doesn't do them properly. Marie feels that Eric does not do his fair share in the store. He often arrives after opening and this does not give them an opportunity to discuss the day's plan before customers arrive.

Last week, in frustration, Marie turned over the books and all the financial aspects of the company to Eric, stating that if he was so unhappy with the way she did things, he could do them himself. They now avoid each other in the store, and also at home.

Marie has busied herself with her son's baseball team, and Eric does not know how to break the impasse. He hates doing the books, and now he feels more frustrated doing a task for which he feels he is not qualified. During their last counseling session, Marie made it clear that she did not want to continue in the business, since Eric had so little appreciation of her skills and abilities.

Eric and Marie share their problem with many couples in business together. Eric has not clearly communicated that he becomes fearful about their financial status

## SAMPLE #4
## JOB DESCRIPTION

| | |
|---|---|
| 1. Job title | Use job titles that clearly say what the person in that position is responsible for. |
| 2. Department or section that the job belongs to | If your company is large enough to have different divisions, this should be set out in the job description. |
| 3. Hours/days of work | State clearly what the hours of work for this position are expected to be. In the case of management or senior management positions, this is not necessary. |
| 4. A summary or purpose statement | Why does this job exist? In one sentence, what is the person in this position expected to accomplish? |
| 5. Reporting relationships and scope of authority | Which positions report to this one? What is the level of authority of this position? |
| 6. Key tasks/functions | What is this position responsible for? Any regular duties and responsibilities should be listed in this section. |
| 7. Required education, experience, and skills | Be sure you are complying with all applicable labor laws and that your qualifications are valid. |

when he doesn't feel the deposits are done properly. He needs to clarify why he reacts the way he does and to let Marie know what would help him. Marie must clearly tell Eric how important it is to her that he arrive for their meetings, since she does not want to make decisions on her own and feels that Eric's lack of attendance indicates a lack of interest.

With counseling, perhaps Eric and Marie can re-clarify what they want to do in the business. Perhaps Marie never wanted to be responsible for the banking. It would be helpful for them to redefine their tasks and responsibilities, and they must also re-visit why they started this business together. They have lost their vision and they are lost in negativity.

# 5
## RESOLVING CONFLICT

### a.  WHAT CAUSES CONFLICT?

There is one thing we know is true in businesses operated by couples. If there is conflict in their lives, it transfers from home to business and business to home. Conflict does not disappear because you leave your house and go to the office. Any unresolved conflict will follow you from home to work and back again, until you and your partner can find a solution.

Conflict arises in couple-operated businesses when —

(a)  You have different goals

(b)  Your beliefs about the business are different

(c)  Your perception of the issue or problem is different

(d)  Your emotional needs are not the same

(e)  You have limited money, time, or other resources

(f)  You have undefined roles and responsibilities

(g)  Your basic ways of doing things are different

Some conflict is healthy. It can lead to new ideas and stronger relationships. But for couple-operated businesses, conflict must be resolved for the business to survive. If you avoid conflict, resentments build up and eventually lead to spectacular explosions. Unresolved conflict increases the stress in your family and your business. Your conflict management style in your business is a reflection of how you resolve conflicts at home.

The first step is to find out where there are areas of conflict, and then build a plan to resolve them. Schedule one hour of uninterrupted time with your spouse or partner to do the following exercise.

Each of you write a list of the areas in which you have different views on how to do things or on how situations should be handled. Be sure to include items on both the home and the business front. You may, for example, have a different view than your spouse does of how sales calls should be conducted. You may think that vendors should wait 90 days to be paid, and your spouse may be uncomfortable with owing money for that long.

If you are not sure of your partner's opinion about something, write it on your list with a question mark. Unless you know for sure how the other person feels, there is a potential area of conflict.

There are five possible resolutions for any conflict:

(a) Win-lose: My way or no way; what I say goes.

(b) Lose-win: O.K. have it your way; I lose.

(c) Lose-lose: If I can't have my way, neither can you.

(d) Standoff: You do your thing, I'll do mine.

(e) Win-Win: Let's look for a solution that benefits us both.

You will find that the resolution you want often depends on how strongly you believe in something. For issues of little importance it is easy to compromise, to give more than you get. But there are other issues that you will fight tooth and nail to protect. It is important to know which is which.

Now, choose one area where you think there is conflict. The questions in Worksheet #4 can help you analyze the area of conflict.

# WORKSHEET #4
## ANALYZING CONFLICT

1. Where do you each stand on this issue? Ask each other to state all of your opinions, feelings, and beliefs about it.

_____

_____

_____

_____

_____

2. What is the common ground (if any) that you share about this issue?

_____

_____

_____

_____

_____

3. What are your fears or concerns about this issue?

_____

_____

_____

_____

_____

4. What are your assumptions about how your partner
   feels/thinks?

   _____

   _____

   _____

   _____

   _____

5. If this issue were resolved to your satisfaction (each person),
   what would be happening?

   _____

   _____

   _____

   _____

   _____

## b. REACHING A COMPROMISE

When you have analyzed the issue, look for common threads or themes and for areas of possible compromise or shared solutions. Test these solutions against the reality of the situation to be sure they will work. If you have any unresolved feelings or emotions, do not agree to the solution because you will not be able to live with it in the long term. If you can brainstorm more than one solution, you will both feel as though you have some choices. You can then evaluate the solutions and decide on the best one. Remember, plan how the solution you have chosen will be implemented, and make a date for a review of how things are going.

### Learning to compromise

Carson and Laura had built their construction company to the point where they were ready to hire a new sales-person to call on corporate accounts. Carson interviewed several people. One of the candidates was an aggressive young man that Laura had met several times at social functions with clients. Carson was very enthused about the possibility of Tim working with them, but Laura was not as excited.

Within two weeks of Tim being hired, Laura had fielded three complaints about his aggressive style. When she confronted Carson with the problem, he refused to see her point of view. He felt that Tim's style was just what the business needed in order to grow. He pointed out that Tim had brought in two huge new accounts in those two weeks. Carson felt that the clients who complained just couldn't adjust to change.

Laura passionately believed that their business depended on good service and good relationships with their existing clients. While Carson agreed, he put more emphasis on building new clients. Carson and Laura agreed to meet with Tim once a week to discuss his plans for the week. Laura would suggest an approach for existing clients since she knew them well, and Tim would describe his plan for new accounts. After they agreed on what approach to take, Tim would complete his sales calls for the week.

In a nutshell, here are the eight steps to resolving conflict:

(a) Define the mutual conflict without emotion.

(b) Honestly set aside any past differences.

(c) Generate as many options as possible.

(d) Evaluate the proposed options.

(e) Decide on the most workable option.

(f) Build an action plan to implement the solution.

(g) Keep your agreements; implement the solution as agreed.

(h) Follow up and review.

Conflict is often generated because of unclear communication. If you keep each other informed of what you think about issues and problems, conflict can be kept to a minimum.

If you find that there are simply too many issues where you disagree strongly, perhaps you need to re-evaluate whether or not you should work together. Money and business is a poor substitute for family. Remember to have some fun, in the business and at home. Keep conflict in perspective. It always helps to be able to laugh at the little upsets that we all have in our lives.

### Taking time out

Inge and Bob had just completed a marathon negotiation session with their suppliers. As an independent travel agency, they needed to work closely with representatives of different airline and tour operators to ensure they could offer competitive rates to their customers. Inge had spent many hours writing proposals, and Bob had been in the air more than on the ground in the last two months. Their children had been cared for by Inge's mother, but things were getting tense at home, too.

Although there was still one week of intense negotiation ahead of them, Bob realized that they needed to replenish their love for each other and their energy as a family. He arranged to pick the children up from their grandmother's house, then he met Inge at the office. Ignoring their protests and questions, he drove the children to a nearby waterslide park, registered them at the motel for two days, and raced the children to be the first one to change into a swimsuit. The only rule for the holiday, to which they all agreed, was that for two days no one was allowed to mention the business. When they returned to the city two days later, the sparkle had returned to their eyes.

## c. HOW NOT TO DEAL WITH CONFLICT

There are some responses to conflict that are not helpful and only make things worse. If they are already a part of your relationship, they may carry over into your business. If you or your partner do tend to respond in these ways, you need to pay special attention because the consequences for your business can be devastating.

### 1. Never use force or threats

If you resort to force, whether emotional or physical, you may achieve short-term results. Threats or emotional blackmail are sometimes used even though you do not intend to follow through. When you force your partner to do something against his or her will, you do so at the cost of your relationship. Over time, these incidents pick away at the fabric of your lives, and the cost can be severe.

### Why threats won't work

Mary and Peter had hired a receptionist for their dental practice some six months earlier. Mary became concerned that the receptionist was undermining her requests and going behind her back to Peter if she didn't like what Mary said. Mary asked Peter to support her in terminating the employee, but since Peter did not share her view of the problem, he refused.

Within two weeks this conflict had escalated to the extent that Mary suggested to Peter that perhaps she, not the receptionist, should quit, and threatened to do just that if Peter did not terminate the employee within the week. When termination did not take place, Mary did not come to work for three days. When this still did not affect the situation, she threatened again to leave the business. In an emotional moment, Peter asked her to make good her threat. Mary and Peter have entered therapy, and the future of their business is uncertain.

### 2. Don't withdraw

Don't take your toys and go home, emotionally or physically. You will become bitter and apathetic, and this will directly affect the energy and enthusiasm you bring to the business. Work toward a real solution, one that restores your sense of participation and commitment.

### Withdrawal symptoms

Ron had repeatedly asked Yvonne to help him design their new layout for the store. She was a talented designer, and could have easily completed drawings in one afternoon. Yvonne was angry with Ron, however, for making a buying decision which she felt left her out of the loop. For two weeks she had been pretending to be too busy to do the designs, and the deadline for approval at city council was near. When Ron asked Yvonne to explain what was troubling her, she simply said she felt too stressed to creatively contribute to new designs. In fact, she took four days off and the deadline for submission passed.

### 3.   Don't involve a third party

Work it out with each other. Don't involve your friends, family, or employees in your conflict. Keep your feelings and opinions about your spouse to yourself. If you talk about your partner with others, you undermine his or her credibility, and this further damages your relationship. If you must involve a third party, make sure it is a business counselor, a therapist, or some other professional who is qualified to give objective views about the situation.

### Don't make employees take sides

When Mary could not get Peter to support her decision to terminate the receptionist, she began to worry that they might be involved with each other. She and another employee, the dental hygienist, were on close terms, and they often discussed the situation. Mary would regale her colleague with stories about conflicts she had with Peter and how the receptionist might be coming between them. This created friction between Peter and his hygienist and further aggravated an already uncomfortable situation.

Remember, with clear roles and responsibilities, you can trust your partner to make decisions in his or her area of expertise. You don't need to become involved, except to understand and support why the decision was made. In turn, your partner will trust you to make decisions in your own areas of responsibility. This lessens the possible sources of conflict between you, and allows you to have the emotional resources you need when an issue needs to be resolved.

# 6

## DECISION MAKING

### a. THERE'S MORE THAN ONE WAY TO DO SOMETHING

**Two people, two different styles**

Tony and Gloria were as different as night and day. To Gloria, when it came time to make a decision, the right one was always immediately obvious to her. She never hesitated, whether it was to terminate an employee or sign her daughter's report card. In her mind, decision making was simple and quick. If there were any negative repercussions, she simply dismissed them as unimportant.

Tony, on the other hand, was deliberate and cautious in making decisions. He needed time to think things over, and he only expressed his opinion when asked. The company had grown to the point where Tony and Gloria needed to hire a manager. This new employee would report to Tony and eventually free him to build other parts of the business.

In her usual straightforward style, Gloria had no difficulty deciding who they should hire and how much they should pay. She was surprised and angry when the new employee quit after two weeks, citing confusion and frustration about who ran the company.

This pattern was a familiar one for Tony and Gloria. Although they had been in business together for 15 years, it was a roller coaster of emotion. Decisions made by Gloria were often made over the protests of others, and

Tony seemed to put off making decisions until Gloria had to take over and make on-the-spot choices. Now that their business was expanding to include several new employees, this style of decision making would no longer work for them.

On a personal or professional level, people adopt different decision-making styles. These vary on a scale from rigid and autocratic to flexible and participative. Some people make decisions quickly, while others require time and large amounts of data to come to their decisions. There is no one style that is appropriate in every situation, although couples tend to use the style with which they are most familiar and comfortable.

Just as entrepreneurial couples define tasks and responsibilities, they can also build a consistent strategy for making decisions. Gloria needs to learn not to make quick, on-the-spot decisions except in clearly defined circumstances. Tony needs to learn that caution can be useful, but sometimes spontaneous decisions are required. Again, it is important for them to know when they can revert to their familiar styles and when it is time to use flexible styles of decision making. Gloria's style works well in short, tight situations where quick thinking is required, but not in situations that require full support or spending company money or time. Tony's style, on the other hand, would not be effective in a crisis situation or when an employee needed an authoritative, leadership decision.

Here are some of the factors couples need to consider when making a decision and the style associated with each factor:

(a) Is this decision completely within the area for which I am responsible? *(Autocratic)*

(b) Will anyone else be affected by the results of my decision? *(Participative)*

(c) Do I have enough information to make the decision on my own? *(Consultative)*

(d) Will I need to consult someone for information? *(Consultative)*

(e) Even if this turns out badly, do I want support from my spouse/partner? *(Participative)*

(f) Is this decision likely to require the use of our company/family resources (money, time)? *(Participative)*

(g) Is it important that everyone support this decision and act on it consistently? *(Participative)*

(h) Is this an emergency? *(Autocratic)*

From time to time it may become necessary to deviate from the planned strategy for decision making, but once couples have a plan they must try to stick to it. Otherwise, there could be nasty results.

### When two styles clash

Arlene and Marty have agreed that she is responsible for all purchasing decisions within their mail order business. She decides what to stock and how much inventory to hold. Recently, Marty was on a business trip and met a supplier with a product that Marty felt would be perfect for their business. The supplier offered Marty a superb deal. Marty phoned Arlene, and she responded quite curtly that he should do whatever he wanted. Marty made the deal with the supplier. When the first shipment arrived, Marty was disappointed with the product and Arlene's pointed "That's what you get for not looking into things," did not help.

Marty has an autocratic, quick-response decision-making style, and this causes him to react by making a decision even on areas that are not his responsibility. Since he did not consult Arlene, he was left to handle the consequences of a decision that did not turn out. In this case, the very least he needed to do was consult Arlene before jumping in. Since that didn't happen, Arlene and Marty now need to discuss how they will handle these kinds of situations in the future. Will Arlene just live with Marty's style and laugh off his "off-the-cuff" decisions, or will Marty learn to temper his quick reactions with "Let me get back to you"? Either method would work, but this problem must be discussed between them.

It is important that couples support decisions without reservation. Don't hold back on your input to a decision. You will both have to live with the results, and it is not fair or productive to complain about a decision if you did not choose to say your piece during the decision-making process. If you find yourself in a situation where the best you can do is compromise, accept that fact and act as if the decision was made with your full cooperation.

There is a Catch-22 situation when it comes to entrepreneurs and decision making. By definition, successful entrepreneurs like to make their own decisions, and they are not very good at consulting others. In a couple-owned business or in a family, however, it is imperative that consultation and participation be the types of decision making that are used. The good news is that couples can learn these different styles, and with practice they become easier. There are many excellent one- or two-day workshops available for entrepreneurs. Couples should make this type of training a regular investment for themselves, their employees, and their families.

You can use Worksheet #5 to analyze your decision-making style and determine where your strengths and weaknesses are.

## b. RECOGNIZING AND DEALING WITH EMOTION

One of the most difficult hurdles for couples to overcome when making decisions is an emotional hurdle. If either partner has a particularly strong personal tie to an issue, this

# WORKSHEET #5
## ANALYZING YOUR DECISION-MAKING STYLE

1. Think of a decision that you and your partner recently had to make that affected the business in a significant way. Write it down in point form.

   _____

   _____

   _____

2. Who had the final say in the decision?

   _____

   _____

   _____

3. Was this

   ☐ Consultative

   ☐ Participative

   ☐ Autocratic

4. Would you both describe this as your normal process for decision making?

   _____

   _____

   _____

5. What kinds of decisions have you made differently? Did they turn out better/worse?

   _____

   _____

   _____

6. What kinds of decisions do you have the most problem making? Could it be because of the style you are using?

_____

_____

7. Analyze the strengths and weaknesses of your style.
   Strengths:

_____

_____

   Weaknesses:

_____

_____

8. On what types of decisions do your styles tend to clash? Can you assign those areas of responsibility to one person to prevent this clash?

_____

_____

9. How could you improve your decision-making style(s) to be more effective in your business?

_____

_____

can cloud the whole process and make it an emotional roller coaster rather than a sound business discussion. It is important that couples are able to define the actual problem that needs to be resolved so that emotion plays a minimal role in the decision.

### Emotions can affect decisions

John's daughter, Carley, wants to work in the store after school. John and Cathryn have owned their business for two years and have been married for three. Carley is 16, and has had a difficult time building a relationship with her stepmother. Cathryn believes that Carley is stealing from her purse whenever she comes to stay with them, and she believes that this behavior would continue in the store. John does not believe this of his daughter, and feels the training would be good for Carley. Cathryn and John cannot rationally discuss what should be done because every time they try to solve this problem, Cathryn becomes angry and loses control. John reacts to her accusations of his daughter, and the decision is once again stalled.

Here is a step-by-step process for Cathryn and John to use to separate the emotion from the problem:

(a) Define the problem. What specifically needs to be decided? What is not part of the problem? What information do you have? How do you feel about the decision you are facing? In this case, the problem is whether or not Carley should be allowed to work in the store. The circumstances under which this should be allowed must be discussed, and Cathryn must be able to state her worries about this arrangement.

(b) Gather information. Do you know anyone who has faced a similar decision? What resources are available to make this decision? Who do you need to consult for help? Cathryn and John might be able to talk to

Carley's mother, or to a school counselor, or to another staff member about this problem.

(c) Predict the future. Imagine you've made the decision. Visualize a future with the decision, and visualize the alternate future. How does each scenario feel to you? Cathryn and John may visualize themselves having a positive impact on Carley's development by having her in the store.

(d) Analyze the pros and cons. Write them down and list the costs and benefits of each. What road blocks might you encounter? How can you get around them? Is the idea worth pursuing? Is there an alternative you have not discovered? In John and Cathryn's case, they must make a provision for close supervision of Carley in the store. If this is not possible, perhaps the decision will have to be not to employ her.

(e) Build an action plan. Make sure it relates clearly to the results you want. Establish time lines and targets. Set accountability. Make sure your plan is flexible enough to allow for surprises. In this case, Carley should be evaluated regularly and made accountable for her sales and her other tasks.

Successful entrepreneurs are often people with a highly individual, risk-taking, egoistic style. They feel strongly about issues and ideas and will argue their position until they win. This type of behavior is not helpful to successful couple-owned businesses where compromise, logic, objectivity, and commitment are required for clear decision making.

# 7
## DELEGATION

### a. IT CAN BE LEARNED

Most management books agree that effective delegation is a key skill required to achieve results. Delegation is defined as "getting things done through others." In traditional employee-employer relationships, people expect a certain amount of work to be delegated to them, and they accept their obligations to complete that work in the time agreed. If the work is not completed on time or up to standard, consequences result that may motivate the employee to achieve the goals as agreed.

In most couples, delegation is an informal process that relies heavily on the cooperation of the partners for success. Requests such as "Would you do me a favor, please?" often achieve the needed result, and only because the other person is willing to participate in the process. If one or the other partner is too busy, or is not immediately available, the goal cannot be achieved unless the requesting partner does the work.

At home, we often informally delegate work to our spouses and children. We say "Please clean your room," or "Would you go to the store for me, please?" or "Take out the garbage," and so on. Again, whether our requests are carried out depends on our family's cooperation, and as many parents can report, this cooperation is not always forthcoming. When the initial request fails, parents resort to offering a variety of "carrots" to achieve the goal. If rewards do not have the desired result, they may have to be replaced with threats. Sometimes, couples use carrots in their businesses as well.

### I'll do yours if you do mine

Debbie and Faraz have a network marketing company that sells home and personal security products. They have done very well and have recently been invited to speak about home security at a new townhouse development opening near them. Debbie has been dreading the idea of standing in front of a group of strangers and speaking, but Faraz is quite insistent that she do the speech. Debbie knows that Faraz really hates to walk the dog in the mornings and, although it will add severe pressure to an already tight morning time frame, Debbie volunteers to walk the dog for the next two weeks if Faraz will give the speech.

When couples work together, the informal style of dele gation used in a relationship can lead to problems. In business, tasks are more than favors — they are essential to the success of the enterprise. Deadlines must be met, standards maintained, and plans must be made for the future.

### Never assume anything

Sean and Joanne own a busy veterinary practice. They have overcome many challenges and looked forward to their first vacation together. When they returned from their three-week voyage, they found the practice in an uproar. They had arranged for the receptionist to run the office, and they asked their 17-year-old son, Patrick, to help out when needed. But the receptionist hadn't been able to come in that week, so that left Patrick in sole charge.

The veterinarian who was filling in was angry about the lack of support and information she had been given. A loyal customer complained about their son's rudeness and threatened to take her business elsewhere. Sean was furious with Joanne, and the soothing effects of the vacation were soon lost.

When Joanne met with the employee she had left in charge, it soon became clear that she was overwhelmed by the task. When Sean and Joanne were around, she could ask questions and thereby appeared to be in control and to know what needed to be done. Joanne assumed this to mean that she could leave her in charge of the entire practice, and found to her dismay that this was far from the truth. Joanne realized that this employee needed a lot more training and guidance.

Patrick, though he has an aptitude and a keen interest in being a veterinarian, had been swamped by his new responsibilities and did not have the experience or wisdom to deal with the many situations that arose. Though he had not been given any instruction about answering the telephone, he had managed to field people's questions and keep track of the appointments. When asked why he had been rude, he explained that he had had four other calls waiting and five clients lined up in the office. He felt he hadn't been rude, just in a hurry.

Joanne and Sean were relieved to hear this; Joanne was able to smooth things over with the client. She said "I'm sorry my son was abrupt with you, but you wouldn't believe what he had to handle. I'm so proud of him." Both parents felt that Patrick had coped very well. They realized that he was someone they could rely on, and with proper training and instruction, especially about the telephone, he was going to be a valuable asset to their practice. They promised themselves that this wouldn't be their last vacation, and that if they devoted some time to training their receptionist and Patrick, they'd be able to have a holiday again soon.

As with all of the skills described in this book, couples can learn the basics of good delegation and apply these skills to their business and to their relationship. Both will benefit from a change. The business will operate more efficiently.

Employees will more clearly understand the tasks to be accomplished, and the results will be consistent and long-lasting. Effective delegation also improves family performance of tasks. If children are given clear guidelines about required results, they can more easily achieve them and contribute more fully to the family organization.

If couples have spent time developing clear job descriptions and are aware of the strengths and weaknesses of each other and their employees, effective delegation is an easier skill to master.

Delegation is *not* an opportunity to get out of doing unpleasant tasks. It is *not* an opportunity to give work that you do not want to someone else. At home or at work, delegation is subject to abuse if it is seen as an opportunity to shirk your responsibilities.

## b. WHAT IS EFFECTIVE DELEGATION?

Even though you and your spouse run the company, there are times when one of you needs to be doing a particular task. Even if your partner has the idea, he or she may not have the skills to bring it to fruition. Or, you may have an employee who would be better suited to a particular task than either of you.

Effective delegation means you must give up some control and develop trust in your partner and your employees. If you find yourself overwhelmed with deadlines at home and at work, it could be a signal that you are not making use of delegation as a management tool.

Here are some excellent reasons to delegate:

(a) There is someone (spouse or employee) who can do the task better than you can.

(b) There is someone who can do the task and gets paid less than you do; therefore, the cost of the task or the performance is lower.

(c) There is someone who can do the job today because you won't be able to get at it for a few days or weeks.

(d) There is someone who wants to learn a new skill, and delegating this task would help in that goal.

(e) There are other priorities for you right now, and you need to learn to delegate and trust your partner or employees.

Delegation is not a hit-and-miss process; rather, it is a two-way conversation with some clear and logical steps.

People who are one-half of a couple-owned business sometimes make assumptions about what their partner has understood, or think he or she has the same vision for the outcome of a particular plan. Effective delegation makes no such assumptions — with partners or employees. For delegation to be successful, the task must have been accomplished to the satisfaction of all concerned.

## c. RESPONSIBILITY FOR MISTAKES

When you delegate a task, you retain responsibility for the result. In couple-owned enterprises, it is essential that both partners understand that each of them is still entitled to make a mistake, even though each of them has accepted the responsibility for achieving a certain result. Delegation is not an opportunity to dump blame on your partner when a project doesn't turn out. You are still accountable for the final result, and if you use all of the steps in effective delegation, you will minimize the likelihood of disaster.

### Use mistakes as an opportunity to train

When Anne asked her assistant to prepare a quote for a large conference, she assumed that Julie knew what to do since they had worked on so many of them together. When the task was complete, Julie asked Anne if she would read the quote. Anne was very busy in negotiations for a major international symposium, and George, her partner/husband, was out of town.

Anne instructed Julie to mail the quote. When the client accepted the bid, Anne discovered that the quote would cost the company $1,200 because of inaccurate information that Julie provided. Anne apologized to the client, and helped Julie research ways to meet their promises within budget. She also assured Julie that in the future she or George would look over all quotes and help Julie prepare them to ensure that they would all look professional.

Disappointment, discouragement, and misunderstandings can be prevented if you follow these five rules for effective delegating:

(a) Define the task.

(b) Choose the right person.

(c) Choose the right time.

(d) Set checkpoints and deadlines.

(e) Give credit and recognition.

## 1. Define the task

Define the task. What needs to be done? What is the deadline date and time? What is the scope of the task? What does excellent performance look like?

If you are delegating a large project, be prepared to describe its pieces so it is not overwhelming to the person who must achieve the result. Don't keep all of the fun jobs for yourself. Make sure that you evenly delegate both the tough and dirty jobs and the interesting, challenging ones.

## 2. Choose the right person

Choose the right person. Does the person have the skills and abilities to perform the task? How do you know? Does the person need any training to do the job? Do you have time to provide the training? Does the person have the interest and motivation to complete the task to your satisfaction?

While we cannot always do only those jobs we like, you can expect better results if the job can be delegated to someone who really wants to do it.

### The right person

Earl was a polished, professional employee, and Margaret had been admiring his performance for many months. They had talked about future growth for Earl within the company, and now she had a project that she felt would help him demonstrate his readiness for promotion. Margaret and Lawrence had built their cleaning company into an operation worth several millions of dollars, and they now felt they had the power to re-negotiate the cost of their cleaning supplies with their largest supplier.

Margaret asked Earl to schedule an appointment with the supplier and handle the negotiation. Two weeks later when she checked with him, he had not done anything about it. This continued until the deadline for the new year's contracts had expired, and the company was forced to sign a contract at the previous, higher rate. Margaret was furious and asked Earl to explain himself. She quickly discovered her error. While Earl enjoyed being a support to Margaret and Lawrence, he was terrified of being in the spotlight. He could quietly and competently hold down the fort in the company, but he could not manage the idea of representing the company in negotiations.

### 3. Choose the right time

Choose the right time. Don't delegate something with such a tight time frame that the person has no chance of success. Do crisis jobs or tasks yourself rather than expecting another person to rescue you from the situation. Be sure to allow enough time to fully explain the task and answer any questions. Choose a time when you can give full explanation of the task, deadlines, and standards to be achieved.

**Wrong time**

Tracy and Rick had been working for two months to prepare a proposal for a European client who wanted to open a franchise in their home town. They were leaving to meet with the client in two days. Just before they left for the airport, Rick called the temp who was filling in for them answering the phone to let her know about a contractor who would be coming to measure their house for renovations. He asked her to let him in and get on with it. When they returned from their trip, the contractor had begun the renovations without approval. The temp only remembers being told to tell the contractor to get on with the job.

### 4. Set checkpoints and deadlines

Don't wait until the final deadline to check the progress of the job. Build a check-in schedule so that you can be informed early if there is going to be a problem or a delay. Be careful not to over supervise people who are competent to do the job, but check in with even the most competent people from time to time.

### 5. Give credit and recognition

When your employee, spouse, partner, or child has successfully completed a task, recognize him or her for the accomplishments. Two of the most powerful words in management are "thank you." Be specific in your praise, stating clearly what you appreciate most about the person's efforts. Let him or her take credit for a job well done, and that person will be more likely to take responsibility when things don't proceed so smoothly.

**Giving credit**

In their creative writing company, Janet and Paul had recently been asked to prepare an annual report for a major corporation. They subcontracted the graphics to a talented young designer and included her in their meetings. The report was so effective and visually appealing that they entered it into a contest and it received second prize. They asked the designer to represent them at the awards dinner and accept the prize, since her graphics had contributed so much to the overall effect.

Effective delegation takes practice. In the early stages, we often fear that if we delegate we will lose control. The corollary of this fear is that if we retain too much control, we will run out of time, energy, and personal resources. We also begin to build a bank of resentment because nobody will help us. Delegation is a signal to our partner, our children, or our employees that we respect their abilities and want them to use their skills on this particular project. It acknowledges that we are not able to do everything ourselves, and sets the tone for strong team participation.

To analyze your business and discover areas where you need to delegate, turn to Worksheet #6.

# WORKSHEET #6
## DELEGATION

1. Define the project. What result are you expecting?  Give
   details and deadlines. If the project is very large, define
   each part and the order in which they should be done.
   What support is available to the employee if he or she
   requires it?

   _____

   _____

   _____

   _____

   _____

   _____

   _____

   _____

   _____

2. Why did you choose this person? List the skills/abilities
   this person has that can be applied to the task. If this is a
   training project, define the skills you would like the person
   to learn. Check the availability of time and the interest
   and motivation level of the person around this project.

   _____

   _____

   _____

   _____

   _____

   _____

   _____

   _____

   _____

3. Checkpoints and deadlines. When do you want to meet to discuss progress? When do you want to be informed about problems? What decision-making authority does this person have before he or she must check in with you?

_____

_____

_____

_____

_____

_____

_____

_____

4. Recognition and reward. What's in it for the employee to do this task? How will you recognize and reward his or her participation?

_____

_____

_____

_____

_____

_____

_____

_____

# 8

## WHEN WORKING TOGETHER ISN'T WORKING OUT

So what happens if working together is not working out? This is a very common situation for couple-run businesses, as the strains of running a company leave little time for repair and maintenance of your relationship. Too often, couples invest every drop of creative energy they have into the growth of the business, leaving nothing left for each other. The thrill of working together can quickly become stifling and repetitive, especially if the business is turning out to be something different from first planned.

This can be a painful period for each of you as you try to make rational decisions in an emotionally charged situation. These decisions are easier to define and make if you remember that the success of your company depends on the success of your relationship. When the going gets tough, tough decisions need to be made.

## a. WHEN YOU FIRST NOTICE HOW MUCH FUN IT ISN'T

### 1. Keep it private

Never discuss your private relationships with your staff. Find someone else to talk to, perhaps your partner, a personal friend, or an objective third party. Your staff need to rely on you as a strong "united-we-stand" management team, leading by example. When you involve a staff member in your personal problems, you put him or her between you and your partner, and make that person choose sides in your dispute, something that sets a precedent for the course he or she will have to take in the future. You are in effect, training your staff to "divide and conquer" the management team as a strategy when disputes arise.

## When personal problems affect business

"I first realized the impact that our personal problems were having on the staff when the bank called to ask me why so far three of our staff had asked to have their paychecks certified from our bank," explains owner Judy. "Although sometimes my husband's and my disagreements got loud and uncomfortable, I never guessed that the staff would think that our problems would translate into job problems for them. To top it all off, now our bank is nervous and wants some kind of reassurance that the company is not in any danger."

## 2. Try to identify what you are unhappy with

Are you unhappy with the job that you are responsible for or the way you have to do your job? Is your unhappiness really caused by the person you work with, or would you be just as dissatisfied if the faces were changed? Identifying the cause of your dissatisfaction is the key to finding a workable solution.

## Working it out

Dave and Linda were increasingly uncomfortable working together. Linda found his lack of detail frustrating; Dave found Linda's demands for perfection annoying. They knew that they needed to deal with their situation and decided that their best approach would be to schedule some time away from the office to work it out.

"As we talked, it turned out that Linda wasn't really unhappy with me or how I approached things, she was really feeling trapped," Dave explains.

"I was tired of being the one to catch Dave's mistakes and knowing that there was nobody checking my work. The pressure to produce perfect work was making me really unhappy" Linda clarifies. Dave and Linda decided to switch some of their job tasks so that Dave reviewed his work for mistakes before it went to Linda, and he set aside some time to check over Linda's work when she requested it.

## 3. Examine the job tasks

If your job is causing the dissatisfaction, then take a look at the tasks each of you do and consider switching the responsibilities around. Many couples find that switching job responsibilities provides a break from routine and an invaluable opportunity to really understand their partners' view.

### Switch roles and duties

"Every year my wife and I switch the role of president and controller. This has worked to really open up my eyes to how frustrating her work is and shows her that being president is not exactly a piece of cake," says Kevin. "I always thought that her job as financial controller would be relatively easy, because it was predictable and straightforward. I had no idea of the scope of her skills or the needs she had for accurate information."

Susan explains: "Switching roles gives us each a chance to really appreciate the intricacies of the job and allows us to expand our skills. While initially the switching was hard, now I look forward to escaping from one job to another."

## 4. Keep talking, even when it gets uncomfortable

Now is the time to practice your conflict resolution skills by separating the people from the issue and working together to solve the problem.

Never underestimate the words "I'm sorry" and "you're right." Many times a clear and rational discussion cannot take place until both parties feel that they will be listened to and respected, and this can start with an apology and a commitment to listen.

### 5. Be willing to negotiate and compromise

Be willing to negotiate and give up ground. You have a lot invested in working it out.

#### Keep talking

"I was getting really tired of always having to fight for and justify my opinions with Don. It felt as though every time I had something to say he would shoot me down or wave me off," says Kim. Eventually Kim and her husband, Don, sought the advice of a professional mediator. "It took us months of mediation to get to the point where we could work together again," says Don. "We ended up splitting up some job tasks and assigning areas of sole responsibility and authority to each of us. This reduces the amount of things that Kim and I have to talk about, and means that when we do talk, it's either after the fact or it's on a point where we must reach consensus. It hasn't been easy, but it's working."

### 6. Get an objective view

Frequently, this is the time to have a third party mediator help you solve the dispute. A mediator can give a clear, objective viewpoint that is unclouded by emotion and unbiased in its observations. Many partnerships rely on mediators to keep the communication rational and fair. Choose this person well in advance, and try to find someone who cares for both of you equally and wants to help you succeed. Mutual business friends, your lawyer, or your accountant can fill this role well because they are familiar with the business and the people behind it. This is not a good role for a family member because he or she can be perceived as being "too involved" to offer objective assistance.

## 7. Find a mediator

Kim and Don found a mediator in the Yellow Pages of their local telephone directory when they went looking for someone to help them solve their communication problems. In this case, the mediator was a specially-trained professional with a background in legal practice. This formal mediator was paid an hourly rate and helped to organize and facilitate Kim and Don's discussions.

Your accountant, lawyer, or outside consultant can sometimes be invited to act as an informal mediator in working out some issues. Whomever you choose as mediator, make sure that all parties agree on the role of the mediator and how involved he or she will be. The ideal mediator is someone who understands how your business works and is committed to helping you reach your goals. Your mediator should not be willing to meet with you unless both of you are present. This approach ensures that all parties are aware of each other's concerns and actions.

## 8. Find a solution

This is the stage where many solutions should be generated by both partners and the mediator. Be flexible and creative when generating options for solutions; there are no limits or boundaries on what you as a couple determine works for you. Your relationship with each other and with the business is what is important here, and you may need to find a solution that is as unique as your relationship.

### An outside perspective

Jack had worked as Tony and Angela's business accountant since they started the business five years ago. As the business grew into three locations and 35 staff members, Jack noticed that Tony and Angela were spending more time arguing over whose responsibility various job tasks were than they were in leading the company. The lack of leadership was beginning to affect their sales.

"As an outsider, it was easy for me to see what was going wrong," Jack explains. "The business was growing so fast that the jobs each of them used to do were now so magnified that they couldn't possibly keep up."

Jack suggested that the three of them meet twice a week and focus on re-structuring Tony and Angela's workload so that they could get back to leading the company. They hired an administrative assistant for Angela, who coordinated the financial information from each of the locations. This freed up Angela to spend more time planning and controlling the budgets, and it helped keep Tony informed with the progress of the overall company.

"Jack helped us to see that our personal problems were caused by the stress of a growing company, and that the increased volume of work was drowning us," Angela points out. "I was running as fast as I could just to keep up, and it seemed like Tony and I never had any time just to talk anymore. With an assistant and Jack's help in looking at things, we were able to make changes that really made a difference."

While solutions vary greatly and depend on the issue they are meant to solve, they generally fall into these categories:

(a) Time flexibility — This gives a partner who feels "trapped" the ability to pick and choose the best times to work and to escape.

(b) Trading tasks — Partners trade job tasks, which has the effect of "rounding out" the skills of each partner and brings new perspectives to old tasks.

(c) Creative communication — Changing the way the two of you communicate about and at work builds a new level of respect and "team" loyalty to each other.

(d) Privacy issues — Scheduling private time together as a couple away from the business and allowing time for each half of the couple to be alone can solve many issues ranging from your personal relationship to stress management and personal development.

## b. WHEN SPLITTING UP IS THE ONLY ANSWER

### 1. What the law says

The legal implications of starting and running a company together is an intricate application of laws, based in part on your marital status, the scope of the breakdown, the legal structure of the business (proprietorship, registered partnership, incorporation), and whether the company has outstanding debts or receivables.

How the split in the management team is handled will have a great, and in many cases, fatal effect on the continued existence of the business and on the personal relationship of the management team. Too often, a couple's relationship has disintegrated past the point of being able to generate solutions and follow a plan of action that allows for the continuation of the business.

The result is that the business usually ends up ceasing operations, the assets are disposed of, and the remaining owners are left to deal with the leftover debts and damages of the company.

### Breakdown

"I knew that I wanted out when I kept making up excuses why I couldn't stay in the office for the day. I just wanted to be anywhere other than working with Lisa at a company I no longer cared about," Mike explains. "It had gotten to the point where we both knew that one of us had to leave, but we couldn't agree on anything, so we kept getting nowhere."

Mike offered Lisa the opportunity to buy him out, but she refused saying that if he couldn't handle his responsibility, then she wasn't going to make it easy for him. As they struggled with the future of their company, sales dropped and employees started to leave. With Mike rarely working, Lisa found herself trying to do the work of two owners and at least one employee. Eventually the bank reacted to the series of worsening financial statements and demanded immediate payment on loans made to the company. Without Mike's assistance and support, Lisa could not gather enough money to appease the bank. The bank moved in and seized the assets of the firm, and sued Mike and Lisa separately for the balance of the loans, as they had each signed personal guarantees and were liable for money owning.

## 2. Have a partnership agreement

Situations such as this happen too frequently in couple-owned businesses that have made no contingency plan for these events. Mike and Lisa should have had a partnership agreement that would govern their actions and detail their responsibilities in a breakup. In this case, a release from any personal guarantees to the bank in the event that one partner leaves would at least have protected Mike from future lawsuits. It would also have helped to have a breakup mediator, such as a lawyer, identified in the agreement. The mediator could have ensured that the agreement was followed and that both parties as well as the company were protected. This is an expensive lesson to learn.

## 3. When the home front breaks down

The breakdown of your personal relationship does not mean that the business has to end, nor does it mean that you have to continue working together as before. How the two of you handle a split depends not only on your communication skills and dedication, but also on the amount and extent of pre-planning you did when you started the business. The time to discuss the "what if it doesn't work out scenario" is at the beginning, when you are determining the structure and responsibilities of your business relationship. It is much easier for you to talk about the "worst case scenario" well before it happens and build a backup plan to deal with it.

In the case of an incorporation, the most likely structure is that the two of you are shareholders and directors, as well as employees of the firm. This means that when a breakup occurs, you need to decide what will happen to the departing party's status as employee, as director, and as a shareholder. These decisions depend primarily on whether or not you want to continue to work together, and if so, how closely. It is important to realize that in the eyes of the law, an incorporation is a living entity and it continues to exist even when the management team changes.

### Making it work

Sandy and Jim knew that it was over. Their relationship had deteriorated to the point that neither was comfortable talking about anything other than the business. Jim found himself putting longer hours in at work and arriving home later each night. Sandy started spending more time working with the employees than ever before, training and re-training them in minor job tasks. They decided that now was the time when one of them should leave the company while the other stayed, so that at least all of their hard work for the last ten years would not go to waste.

Sandy offered to be the exiting party, as she felt that she was not interested in running the company on her own and she had decided to take a full-time job for the next year or so just to "get her bearings." To help them govern the split-up, Sandy and Jim followed the partnership agreement that they had drafted when they started the company. The agreement clearly detailed how Sandy would be reimbursed for her part ownership in the company as well as the timing and amount of the payments that the company was to pay to Sandy.

"Thank goodness we followed the advice of our corporate lawyer all those years ago," Jim says. "We never would have known where to start, and we would have fought every step of the way." Using their lawyer to guide the process, Jim and Sandy managed to keep talking throughout the process. Sandy went on to a full-time job with a large national firm, and she still maintains an advisory position on their company's board of directors.

"Jim and I can actually meet, catch up on the business, and have a nice dinner together," Sandy explains. "Without the stress of working together, and with each of us doing different things, we have a lot of things to talk about and help each other with."

In the case of either a proprietorship or a partnership, the existence and continuation of the business depends solely on what the two of you decide. A partnership cannot exist when one of the partners exits. A proprietorship depends solely on the existence of the proprietor, regardless of any management relationships that they may have.

When you first structure the business, create a document that covers the disposition of the assets and liabilities of the company as well as the roles and responsibilities of each of the parties. In the case of an incorporated company this takes the form of a shareholder's agreement that clearly details what procedures should be followed should a shareholder cease to be involved in the company. In non-incorporated partnerships and proprietorships, this may be a disposition agreement. Whatever the title, this is a legal document that governs the effect that any personal breakup will have on the existence of the business. The document should be drawn up with the assistance of your lawyer and, ideally, your third-party mediator. Here are a few of the areas that your agreement should cover:

(a) The future of your company

(b) Your mediator in any disputes

(c) How assets and liabilities are to be taken care of

(d) Who owns shares

(e) The duties of the partner who leaves the business

While this is by no means an exhaustive list of what can be taken care of in your disposition agreement, it should serve as a guide to what is essential.

As a couple, it is important that you deal with these issues and details before you have to, because once the breakdown occurs, this conversation becomes extremely difficult for even the most dedicated couples to have. Frequently, the process of working out an agreement allows couples to talk about issues that they would not otherwise have considered and can, in fact, result in the business taking a different structure and direction than originally planned. It can also have the effect of each member of the couple determining their level of commitment and dedication to the business in terms of financial investment and risk, time commitment, involvement of other family members, willingness to resolve conflict, and personal ability to handle stress. Worksheet #7 can help you organize your thoughts about what should be in your partnership agreement.

Does this process remind you of a marriage contract? It should. The purpose and the process of developing a marriage contract is very similar to that of producing a disposition agreement, and it can be just as challenging and as creative. Keep in mind that the time to create these agreements and develop your communication skills is during the "honeymoon" stage of your relationship, right when you have decided to start and run a business together. At this point, you both are committed to making your business relationship work by using good communication skills to develop contingency plans.

Agreements you develop before you need them have the effect of creating a foundation of trust that each member of the management team can have for the other. When couple entrepreneurs begin their enterprise by structuring their trust and responsibilities, the resulting business tends to be stronger and more successful.

## WORKSHEET #7
## WHAT SHOULD BE IN YOUR
## PARTNERSHIP AGREEMENT

Both partners must plan for what will have to be done if the working partnership does not work out. Take time now to consider what should be in your partnership agreement. Record your thoughts below or on a separate sheet. Compare your answers with your partner's.

### 1. The future of your company

If your partnership ends, what will happen to the company? Will it be sold, closed, or will it be run by the remaining party? Do you both agree about what should happen? Your decision here will have a profound effect on the rest of the agreement.

_____

_____

_____

_____

_____

### 2. Assign a mediator

Who will be your mediator? Will his or her role be a facilitator, liaison, or referee? Is the mediator responsible for valuing the assets? How will the mediator be paid? When does the mediator's responsibility end?

_____

_____

_____

_____

_____

### 3. Disposal of assets and liabilities

What is to happen with the assets and liabilities of the business? Will the departing party continue to be liable for the debts of the company or will the remaining party take over the personal guarantees of the exiting party? Does the departing person have any rights to the assets or cash of the company?

_____

_____

_____

_____

### 4. Ownership of shares

What happens to the shares of the departing person? Will the shares be kept or will they be sold to the remaining party, and if sold, at what price?

_____

_____

_____

_____

### 5. The role of the exiting party

Will the party who decides to leave continue in the capacity of board member and quarterly adviser, or will he or she simply be a "silent investor"?

_____

_____

_____

_____

# 9

## THE HOME-BASED BUSINESS AND THE FAMILY

### a. BLENDING WORK WITH FAMILY LIFE

The couple-owned business is a rapidly growing trend, and there is a strong indication that it will continue in the future. More and more couples are starting businesses from their homes. Network marketing, mail-order, consulting, and counseling businesses are just some of the businesses that couples have started from their homes. Artists and interior designers can also be home-based.

When you run your business from your home, you face an additional distraction and concern: your children. How do you make time for them? Where is the dividing line between business and family, when both occupy the same space 24 hours a day? For most couples, full-time child care is a luxury. How will you run your business and cope with your children's demands?

The reality of having children in your home-based business must not be underestimated. Whenever there is a decision to be made about the business, it automatically involves the children. When will you do sales calls? Will clients come to your home? What do you do during the middle of a client meeting when a little one demands to be fed?

### Children's needs vs. client's needs

Jennifer and Nick have two children. They run a home-based drapery and window covering business. Their oldest child, Lisa, is ten; she is quite self-sufficient and likes to greet clients when they come to the door. Timmy, their youngest, likes to compete with Lisa over who will get to the door first when a client calls. The children also compete over who will get to the telephone first.

Sometimes the children's battles get very fierce; they yell at each other and push as they rush for the door. Jennifer is often caught in the middle. She has to get up from talking to a client and go and separate the two children. On one occasion, a client asked to reschedule the appointment to a time when the children were at school. The client did not feel able to concentrate on Jennifer's designs with the two children in the house.

As with any other issue that you face in your business, you must plan for the involvement of children in your business. Decide whether you need to build or set up a separate area in your home strictly for the business. Make some agreements with your children about the space, and with your spouse about sharing child care responsibilities.

If you are both in the office, who's minding the children? We met a couple who could not set aside space and the boundaries between business and home were easily blurred. They made an agreement with their young children: when Mommy and Daddy were wearing certain clothes, identified as "business clothes," this meant that they were working and the children must follow the family rules about working hours. When the parents were off work, they dressed in "play clothes." This signalled the end of work and a return to the comfort of family.

When your children are old enough to understand, tell them about your business and explain what you do. Let them watch you work, and help them understand how important it is to treat visitors to your home with respect and courtesy. Set some ground rules for the telephone. If you want your children to answer the telephone, or if you feel you cannot prevent it, teach them what to say. Practice with them daily.

In some businesses such as network marketing, there are no set office hours, so it is better to have your children answer the telephone the same way all the time, even if it turns out to be Grandma calling.

You and your spouse must develop the ability to pay attention to your surroundings. Even if you are working at home, you never stop being a parent. If your partner is on the telephone with an important client and your child runs into your office crying "I'm going to throw up," obviously you can't wait for your partner to hang up just because "it's his (or her) turn."

Dividing child care duties is not as easy as assigning business responsibilities according to your strengths and weaknesses. Each of you will learn to do the many tasks involved, including attending school meetings, bathing dogs, and drying tears.

Many couples become entrepreneurs when their families are already in place. If the business is based in the home, this is a dramatic change in lifestyle for the family. Without proper planning and attention, the stresses of running a business and managing a family surface daily and quickly grow into crisis after crisis.

### Helping children handle the transition

Alan was laid off from his job as an accountant; he received a sizable severance package. Within five days of his termination, he and his wife Jenna decided that this was their opportunity to start their own home-based consulting business. They ordered letterhead, bought computers, wrote a marketing plan, and told all their friends about the new enterprise.

During their first week in operation, their oldest daughter, Jamie, was sent home from school for fighting. Sharon, their seven-year-old daughter, was sleeping poorly and waking up in the middle of the night with bad dreams. Their son Michael, age three, had just been toilet trained but he seemed to have forgotten everything he'd learned. One morning as Alan reviewed a list of possible new clients, Michael stood beside him wailing because he'd wet his jeans. Jamie stormed in and told her brother to be quiet. Alan exploded: "Can't you see we're trying to run a business here! What do you think this is?"

After the ensuing chaos had calmed, Jenna and Alan realized the strain their quick decision to start a business had placed on everyone. The children were confused about why Mommy and Daddy were at home all the time, and frightened by the new energy level in their house. Jenna and Alan decided they needed to begin again with their children and slowly ease them into the idea that they were now running a business from home. They needed to help the children feel part of, not excluded from, that process.

## b. KEEPING EVERYTHING BALANCED

A home-based business can quickly expand to fill all the hours available. Weekends become just two more days to work, evenings are a good time to catch up on paperwork, and as soon as the children are out of the house, the business day begins.

Just because you and your partner are at home doesn't mean that you are spending time with the children. It is imperative that definite times be set aside as time off for you and your family. Time off means time spent away from the business. You need to get out of the house, play together, and recharge your emotional batteries.

When you run your business from your home, you must be adept at juggling many schedules. You can't just dash out of the house to pick up a sample; first you have to make sure that someone is looking after the children. If your spouse is out on a sales call, you will have to take the children with you.

# ORDERING INFORMATION

All prices are subject to change without notice.
Books are available in book, department, and stationery stores.  If you cannot buy the book through a store, please use this order form.  (Please print)
**IN CANADA**
Please send your order to the nearest location:
Self-Counsel Press, 1481 Charlotte Road,
North Vancouver, B. C. V7J 1H1

Self-Counsel Press, 8-2283 Argentia Road,
Mississauga, Ontario  L5N 5Z2

**IN THE U.S.A.**
Please send your order to:
Self-Counsel Press Inc., 1704 N. State Street,
Bellingham, WA  98225

Name_____

Address_____

_____

Charge to:
❑Visa          ❑ MasterCard

Account Number_____

Validation Date _____

Expiry Date_____

Signature_____

❑ Check here for a free catalogue.

Please add $2.80 for postage & handling.
In Canada, please add 7% GST to your order.
WA residents please add 7.8% sales tax.
**YES, please send me**

_____copies of **Preparing a Successful Business Plan,**
$14.95